MEASURE, EXECUTE, WIN

Measure, EXECUTE, WIN!

AVOIDING STRATEGIC INITIATIVE DEBACLES AND KNOWING WHAT YOUR BUSINESS CAN AND CAN'T DO WELL

ALEX CASTRO

LIONCREST
PUBLISHING

MEASURE, EXECUTE, WIN
*Avoiding Strategic Initiative Debacles and Knowing
What Your Business Can and Can't Do Well*

ISBN 978-1-5445-1335-5 *Paperback*
      978-1-5445-1334-8 *Ebook*

Cover design by Michael Nagin
Book design by John van der Woude

To I.C., R.C., and M.M. Just think of all the time you could get back in your lives if only I had written this book sooner. Love you.

CONTENTS

Vision without execution is hallucination.

—Thomas Edison, Henry Ford, and
literally every CEO after them

*It's only by saying "no" that you can concentrate on
the things that are really important.*

—Steve Jobs

INTRODUCTION

Fifty percent of all strategic decisions fail.[1]

Think about the top ten initiatives in your organization today. How confident are you that your teams can move forward on them? Is that confidence, or lack of confidence, based on opinion, past performance, or a hunch?

Great leaders are no longer differentiated by having a vision for the future, innovative ideas, disrupting

---

1   Nutt, Paul, "Half of Business Decisions Fail Because Of Management's Blunders, New Study Finds," *Ohio State News, August 6, 2002,* https://news.osu.edu/half-of-business-decisions-fail-because-of-managements-blunders-new-study-finds/.

markets, understanding their customers, or having the courage to do what others have been afraid to do. These days, the differentiator comes from understanding their ability to execute.

This book is intended to help leaders identify those activities and initiatives that might have great potential but no real chance of delivering on promises.

To do that, leaders need an entirely new kind of metric, one that provides an execution capability (or readiness) score for each initiative being considered. With this information, leaders can balance their decision-making processes toward those initiatives, which they actually have a good chance to execute successfully.

This metric is called the ReM Score™.

You will discover the power and purpose of this game-changing measurement in the coming chapters.

WHY STRATEGIC DECISIONS FALL SHORT

Leaders create a strategy, identify its potential, and largely justify their ability to realize it with biased beliefs that support their vision. Imagine a bank making a loan based solely on your loan application and financials without bothering to check your credit score. Imagine a university that looked at your high school transcripts but didn't bother to check your SAT score. Imagine buying bonds based solely on the reputation of a municipality without ever looking at the bond rating.

When executives don't measure their company's ability to execute on strategies, they lack the necessary data in decision-making to avoid the debacles that slow the growth of their business and erode their return-on-invested-capital (ROIC) ratio, investor and customer confidence.

To thrive in today's "one shot to get it right" market, companies must integrate an *execution capability score* as a core decision-making metric, articulating their ability to implement a strategy—no longer relying on opinion or feeling.

All too often, leaders put out a vision and strategy and then start producing products, buying companies, or moving into new markets with no clear sense of whether or not they actually have the ability to execute on that vision. They tell themselves, "This will take us three, six, or nine months to achieve."

But eighteen months, twenty-four months, or thirty-six months pass, and they haven't achieved their goal. The product misses the window of opportunity. The acquisition falls short in its performance because it failed to integrate into the culture. The company struggles to find footing in the new market. The initiative ends up costing two, three, or four times what they budgeted, and leaders have no idea why.

Suddenly, they are forced to rob Peter to pay Paul in order to bolster earnings because the strategy isn't performing at the level they anticipated. Consequently, they end up piling even more new things on top of the previous strategy in order to create additional growth to meet expectations.

What if, instead, an executive could decide on an initiative with complete confidence because they knew their company had the capacity to deliver? What if leaders, as part of the decision process, measured their ability to execute on each of the initiatives necessary to realize a vision and knew exactly where the gaps were and exactly where the company was vulnerable? What if leaders could approach an analyst call or media event and show that they'd fully measured everything they invested or plan to invest in?

Is such confidence possible? Absolutely, but it requires a shift in thinking. Leaders aren't struggling from a lack of great business ideas. The struggle comes from a gross misunderstanding about their own companies' execution capability of those ideas.

THE DANGERS OF DECISION BIAS

Over the past twenty years, evidence indicates that decision-making biases are killing big businesses.[2] Executives believe they have some special insight—the secret sauce—that enables them to see what others don't see. In reality, they're no more insightful, and no better at predicting success, than your average stockbroker. In other words, they're mostly crossing their fingers and hoping their existing resources can get them there.

However, in many cases, the next acquisition, product launch, new market expansion, or back-office optimization not only has to increase their current numbers, it has to make up for past strategies that did not meet

---

2   Andrew Campbell, Jo Whitehead, Sydney Finkelstein, "Why Good Leaders Make Bad Decisions," *Harvard Business Review, February* 2009, https://hbr.org/2009/02/why-good-leaders-make-bad-decisions.

predicted targets. Failing that, common "go-tos" such as stock buybacks take their place.

In an era of ever-changing strategy and market evolution, companies are struggling to meet expectations. They're falling short on earnings per share (EPS). As of this writing, EPS calculations are negative for more than half of the s&p 500. It costs almost twice as much to get a dollar of earning as it used to.

In many of the companies that are struggling to make their numbers, leaders attempt to fill in the gaps in their understanding. In the absence of data, they bridge those gaps with their own biases, often based on past experience. As a result, they are held back by the very decision-making process that is intended to help them make progress.

It's not the fault of a product manager, or an acquisitions team, or a project management office. By the time the initiative gets to those people, it's already too late, and the company is doing damage control, whether they realize it or not.

> *The heads of many companies are not skilled in capital allocation. Their inadequacy is not surprising because*

most bosses rise to the top because they have excelled in an area such as marketing, production, engineering, administration or, sometimes, institutional politics.

—Warren Buffett, 1987 letter to Berkshire Hathaway shareholders[3]

In the end, the company bleeds money in its attempt to execute a strategy that was set up to fail. To avoid this, leaders have to avoid getting into that position in the first place. They need a new way to approach their biases, strategies, and decisions.

THE RAPID PACE OF CHANGE

No company is safe from the increasing pace of change. Consider the fact that General Electric first entered the s&p 500 in 1897, but they dropped off the list in June 2018. Subsequently, they restructured their management as they scrambled to recover. Sadly, they are just one of many victims of a market that moved too fast without them. The average life of a company in the s&p 500 has gone from seventy-five years to fifteen years.

---

3   Warren Buffett, "To the Shareholders of Berkshire Hathaway Inc." February 29, 1988, http://www.berkshirehathaway.com/letters/1987.html.

In today's digital, subscription-based economy, the pace of change is faster than ever, yet many executives make decisions like we're still in the 1980s. You no longer get two or three chances to make a strategy work. You don't have a year or two to get it right. At most, you get six months, because someone else is going to show up with an idea that negates everything you're working on and torpedoes your investment.

Professor Paul Nutt of Ohio State University conducted a twenty-year study of the government and private sector. His study concluded that more than 50 percent of *all* strategic initiatives fail.[4]

On average, companies budget 10 percent of earnings for strategic initiatives. Half of the money they're spending generates absolutely no value. Let that sink in. Most companies have to generate about $8 in sales in order to accumulate $1 in the bank, so in reality, they're setting fire to $8 in sales for every dollar of earnings every year. It's like the company is eating itself.

Is that what's happening in your company?

---

4 Paul C. Nutt, *Why Decisions Fail: Avoiding the Blunders and Traps That Lead to Debacles*, *(San Francisco: Berrett-Koehler Publishers, 2002).*

A 2013 McKinsey survey found that only 16 percent of board members completely understood how their companies created value.[5] The success of companies that prioritize capital allocation, along with pressure from the investment community, has led to a greater emphasis on ROIC among executives. This trend should increase the efficiency of the capital markets and create opportunities for investors to benefit from improved corporate governance.

What if you could reduce that waste by 25 percent next year, then 50 percent the following year? All of those extra earnings could then go to other successful initiatives or to your bottom line. The execution capability score model presented in this book can help you get there, providing a clearer and more focused understanding of your capabilities. By implementing this metric, you will accelerate your strategies and turn them into reality.

No longer will you have to say, "That was such a great idea. Too bad we couldn't pull it off."

Wouldn't that be amazing?

---

5 David Trainer, "CEOs Who Focus On ROIC (Return On Invested Capital) Outperform," *Forbes, September* 12, 2018, https://www.forbes.com/sites/greatspeculations/2018/09/12/ceos-that-focus-on-roic-outperform.

PART ONE

THE POWER OF MEASUREMENT

CHAPTER 1

GOOD STRATEGY, BAD EXECUTION

As a leader, are you frustrated that you're not moving toward your vision at the pace you want? Do you wonder how you can realize your strategies faster to relieve the pressure and meet expectations for growth?

The culture of innovation in the business world has enhanced how leaders approach the direction of any company, division, or industry. People are a lot less conservative in regard to strategies and decisions, and there's a lot more creative thinking taking place.

Innovation is the oft-repeated management mantra. You hear it at conferences, read it in mission statements, see it listed as a core value in many companies, and hear it in countless keynote speeches. Boards are obsessed with innovation.

As a result, there are a lot of executives expending a lot of energy and passion to generate great new ideas. However, when it comes to the implementation of these cutting-edge, creative ideas, the thinking among executives is practically medieval, particularly in regard to selecting which initiatives to approve. Those same creative executives find themselves sitting in weekly, monthly, and quarterly meetings, measuring the results from their great ideas and finding, to their dismay, that 50 percent of them are failing. The best ideas in the world don't move at the pace they'd hoped for and are consuming far too many resources.

The Quaker Oats Company had a dynamic range of brands that held the number one or two spots for eighty-five of their product categories for many years. As part of their aggressive growth strategy, they acquired Stokely-Van Camp, the makers of Gatorade sports drink, in 1983.

According to analysts, their CEO at the time, William Smithburg, achieved this success largely through luck rather than skill. His decision to buy Gatorade came from trying the product and liking it, since he was an impulsive decision-maker who tended to do what his gut told him. After the acquisition, he managed to grow Gatorade from a $220 million purchase to an asset worth over $3 billion through innovative advertising and positioning, making it the top-selling drink by 1987. This success earned him complete freedom from Quaker's board of directors in making future acquisitions.

Then the Snapple acquisition happened in 1994—a debacle so large that it seriously damaged Quaker and ultimately cost Smithburg his job.[6]

More about that in a minute.

How can such a large company start the year with so much optimism only to find everything falling apart within a few short months? This is by no means an uncommon experience.

---

6   "The Quaker Oats Company History," *Funding Universe, accessed April* 17, 2019, http://www.fundinguniverse.com/company-histories/the-quaker-oats-company-history/.

FEAR OF THE BLACK SWAN

Ultimately, leaders are being hindered by one fundamental thing—they lack the ability to measure and understand their ability to execute on the idea. The idea was creative, innovative, and compelling, but the company simply didn't have the means to successfully implement it.

When leaders meet to discuss innovative initiatives, they don't have a clear way to determine which ideas they have the capacity to realize and which they do not, so they don't know which initiatives to move on and which to leave behind. They choose the idea that seems best—practically a toss of the dice—and then later are confronted with the harsh reality that they can't pull it off.

To understand what this looks like, let's examine Quaker's debacle. CEO William Smithburg's success at taking the Gatorade brand and turning it into what was, and still is, one of the most successful sports drinks in the world drew the attention of consumers, but it also drew the attention of some who began to consider Quaker a takeover target.

Smithburg got hooked on the excitement of turning a small acquisition into a big hit. He assumed he had the "magic formula" for success, a belief which created a clear bias, and, at the same time, he wanted to stave off a possible takeover. To achieve both, he did what he "knew" and acquired Snapple, and no one at his company said a contrary word for fear of what would happen to them if they contradicted a CEO the board had given free rein.

To help fund the acquisition, Smithburg sold off Quaker's successful pet food and baked bean divisions. He never considered raising debt or issuing more stock. All of these decisions were made almost unilaterally with most of the process never being measured or vetted.

No one ever openly asked the question, "Why do we want to avoid a takeover?" After all, with a takeover, shareholder value would have gone through the roof and benefited everyone. The only real problem with an acquisition is that Smithburg would have had a much more controlled role post-acquisition, if any at all. This created another bias that dictated much of his decision-making.

The assumptions that carried into the Snapple deal are what sunk Smithburg. Snapple had no manufacturing or distribution synergies with Gatorade. Snapple distributors had to give up lucrative supermarkets in order to supply smaller outlets, but independent bottlers had long-term contracts with Snapple, while Gatorade was centrally manufactured. Snapple was also carrying more than $20 million in obsolete materials because of poor inventory management.

As things got worse, Smithburg poured more and more money into corrective efforts. Quaker tried to renegotiate contracts to reduce costs, but they overlooked alternatives as they continued to support the CEO's original direction. Smithburg fired any manager who couldn't execute on his corrective plans, even forcing out Philip Marineau, his one-time heir apparent whom Quaker had groomed for twenty-three years. Smithburg's energy, which had once been dedicated outward, was now turned almost entirely inward in an effort to tighten controls.

The huge losses incurred in the Snapple debacle almost brought the entire Quaker company down. Two years after the acquisition, for which Quaker paid $1.7 billion,

Snapple was sold off for $300 million, and Smithburg was forced to step down.[7]

This is just one example of the real danger. Even if you come up with the most amazing idea of all time, an idea that could revolutionize your entire industry, it's useless if you don't have the ability to execute it. If the best idea in the world is going to consume your business, you're better off leaving it behind. If an initiative fails badly enough, it can sink your business and you likely won't recover from its lack of performance.

You might not even realize you can't make it work. Everything in your company might seem aligned for a successful execution, but when you hand the idea off to your team, it turns into a black swan project. Many executive leaders in recent years have been shocked to find that their confidence in a project was in vain, as the whole thing crashed down around them.

In the aftermath of a strategy's failure, some blame executives for not being creative enough, but that is rarely the problem. Many executives are *overflowing*

---

7   Neil Steinberg, "Snappled!" *Chicago Reader, May* 29, 1997, https://
www.chicagoreader.com/chicago/snappled/Content?oid=893549.

with innovative ideas. They have a clear and compelling vision for where they'd like to see the company go and how they'd like to meet market demand. Their ideas aren't the problem. They simply lack the data to know what their execution capabilities are.

BEYOND STRATEGY

Some big companies are beginning to recognize this problem. Netflix has created an open culture presentation that is freely shared on their website, and in that presentation, they reveal a critical conclusion of their own organizational studies. As they have found, with growth comes an increase in business complexity, which makes it harder to avoid chaos. To do so, companies often employ increasingly more stringent processes and lean principles in order to optimize operations.

However, implementing more stringent processes makes it harder to adjust to market changes. When the market shifts, as it inevitably does, companies often find that they can't adapt because of the increased rigidity of their capabilities.

As they say, rigid processes provide seductive near-term outcomes, but when the market shifts due to new technology or competitors or business models, the company finds that it is unable to adapt quickly, because the employees are extremely good at following the existing processes, and process adherence is the value system. The danger then is that the company generally grinds painfully into irrelevance.[8]

Most companies suffer from rigidity in their current people, processes, and technology. Leaders assume they are adaptable, but they lack a clear metric to understand their adaptability. Consequently, they tend to have mistaken notions about what their people and processes can achieve when it comes to future strategic initiatives.

Without realizing it, you might be making strategic decisions without the data you need to be successful. Coming up with a great strategy is the easy part. The hard part is making it happen.

Sometimes, executives try to implement a great idea in their companies, full of excitement and optimism, only to see the idea fail during implementation. The following chart gives us an idea of why this happens.

8   "Netflix Culture: Freedom and Responsibility," *Netflix*, https://jobs.netflix.com/culture, accessed February 22, 2019.

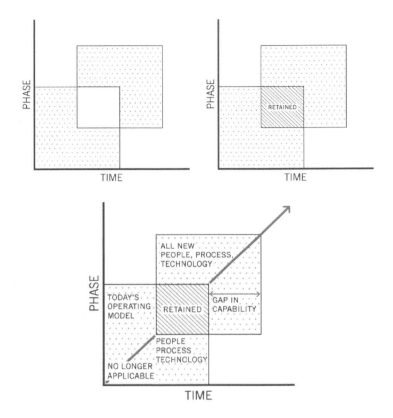

On this chart, the x axis represents time, while the y axis represents the specific phase or iteration of your company, brand, or product in which a strategy is implemented. The shaded block at the bottom represents the existing people, processes, and technology in the company that are optimized today, while the shaded block at the top represents the intended growth that an initiative is meant to achieve.

Essentially, the initiative is meant to move the block up the diagonal line.

The darker block represents the overlap between your current state and the desired future state. It represents your current people, processes, and technology that will still be relevant as they implement the strategy. Everything else in the bottom block will no longer apply and must be replaced to align to the new need. These are the people, processes, and technology that cannot help you execute on that future state. Either the skill-sets are wrong, your processes need to be reengineered, or your technology can't support the implementation. You will need new people, processes, and technology to fill in the gaps for that future state to exist.

The gap between the darker block and the edge of the new intended state represents your gap in execution capability. This is the area that company leaders tend not to measure or pay attention to. They might say, "We have great hiring and retention practices, so we've acquired a bunch of great people," but they don't realize that those great people have a massive gap in their ability to execute the company's strategy, which makes them unable to support the new direction, no matter how great they are.

This isn't a condemnation of their worth as professionals. They simply can't do what the company needs in order to enact strategic growth.

Leaders can't necessarily see or understand the gap in their company in terms of operations, so it becomes an invisible obstacle they keep stumbling over. There is no data to help them recognize that they simply *can't* succeed no matter how good their strategy is. Often, they fill the gap with a belief structure that reassures them of their chances of success.

It's like giving someone a loan without a clear sense of whether or not they will be able to repay it, or hiring an interesting new employee without a clear sense of whether or not they will fit in the company culture.

A TRUE METRIC

What's missing isn't an opinion. "I don't think we should hire this person. I get a sense they won't fit in." What's missing is a true metric. "I *know* she won't fit in, and here is the data to prove it."

In the absence of such a metric, company leaders start moving on an initiative and run into unforeseen issues, so they start adding resources to deal with them. "This is simply a hurdle," they say. "It's a normal part of the process. Let's get past it."

In reality, they are tripping over problems they could have fixed before they even decided to engage in the process. What they're doing is like trying to build an airplane and fly it at the same time. Pieces are falling off midair, and people find themselves doing frantic damage control to keep from crashing.

This leads to a cascade of bad decisions, as well as a desperate search for cause. "It was the project manager, the product manager, the acquisition lead, the market manager, the general manager of the division. They're responsible." The hard truth is that the initiative should never have moved forward in the first place. Before considering implementation, time spent identifying the vulnerabilities and applying corrective actions removes the obstacles often encountered in execution.

MAKING UP LOST GROUND

If you watch the Olympics, you often find that the difference between the winner and loser comes down to tenths of seconds. In any high-level competitive race, you have runners who are side by side, furiously heading toward the finish line, and they might only be five-tenths of a second apart.

At the 1992 Summer Olympics, for example, the top five sprinters in the 100-meter dash crossed the finish line within 6/100th of a second of each other. The winner, American Gail Devers, had a run time of 10.82 seconds, while her fourth-place teammate, Gwen Torrence, finished with a time of 10.85 seconds.[9]

Now imagine a runner coming out of the gate who is pointed three degrees to the right without realizing it. They can't even perceive the three-degree difference at the beginning of the race. It's not until they are far down the track that they realize their misalignment is causing them to fall farther and farther behind the other runners, but correcting the problem now is almost impossible. No matter how much harder they run, they will never make up the difference.

What does the runner do when trying to make up the lost ground? They start pushing harder and harder,

9   Olympic. "USA's Gail Devers Claims 100m Gold In Tight Finish - Barcelona 1992 Olympics." YouTube video, Duration 2:18. Posted October 31, 2011. https://www.youtube.com/watch?v=G-0efltp_Us.

becoming so desperate that they go beyond the bounds of their training. Their strides become more reckless, and they open themselves up to greater mistakes. They are more likely to trip or stumble, so even small obstacles become big problems. Even if they make up for lost time, they still might not be pointed in the right direction.

With the super-pace of markets today, that misaligned gap at the beginning widens very fast, and the cost of correction requires a tremendous amount of resources.

In an article for MIT *Sloan Management Review*, Donald Sull warns about companies sprinting to beat rivals. He writes, "Rushing to execute a flawed plan only ensures that a company will get to the wrong place faster than anyone else."[10] More broadly, Sull concludes, "Beliefs on how to implement strategic initiatives are just plain wrong."

This is a scenario that plays out in countless companies every day. Leaders enact some strategic initiative without realizing they are three degrees off the mark, and by the time they realize they are losing ground,

---

10 Donald N. Sull, "Closing the Gap Between Strategy and Execution," MIT *Sloan Management Review, July 1, 2007, https://sloanreview.mit.edu/article/closing-the-gap-between-strategy-and-execution/.

they become desperate to catch up. This leads to reck-lessness and compounding mistakes, and in many cases, the whole strategy crashes to the ground.

None of this would have happened if they'd had the right alignment coming out of the gate. They would never have found themselves veering off in the wrong direction, losing ground, and desperately trying to catch up.

The problem that is realized well into an initiative has its root cause right around the starting gate. Leaders decide to come out of the gate pointed in a certain direc-tion without having complete clarity. Acceleration comes from taking the time to reorient, *then* start the race. Instead, the pressure to move forward results in spending much of the race trying to course correct before ultimately losing. In the end, initiatives have consumed vastly more energy and resources than they would have if they'd simply taken the time to orient themselves properly beforehand.

I've been a competitive rower since college, so I have experienced this problem firsthand. Anytime you find yourself trying to make up lost ground because of an early mistake, it zaps your energy, because you find yourself not only trying to compete but trying to over-come your own mistake. It's exhausting and discouraging, and it's no way to win.

WHEN CONFIDENCE BIAS TAKES THE PLACE OF DATA

Why aren't leaders considering execution capability at the point of decision? I believe most leaders fear it will slow them down. Taking the time to consider all the factors that might impede the implementation of a strategy seems incredibly time-consuming. Leaders fear the window of opportunity to achieve their objective will pass them by before they can implement their great idea. It's a risk that seems like too much of a variable.

At the same time, leaders are often afraid of what they'll find if they look into their execution capability. It's the same fear people have when they go to the bank for a loan, and the bank says, "Your application is in order, and your personal financials look good, so we're just going to check your credit rating now."

Even someone with good credit will have a moment of anxiety. What if the credit rating comes back and it's far lower than the applicant expected? What if there's been some big problem in their credit history that they're unaware of? No matter how good their personal financial information might be, a low credit rating will put a limit on what they can do.

Knowing this, the applicant is afraid. In a similar way, many company leaders are afraid of what an execution capability metric will show, because they don't want anything to interfere with the opportunity they perceive in the market. Though this should be all the more reason to look into it, they shy away.

At the same time, leaders have been trained their entire professional lives to operate with a mindset of confidence. It's why they are leaders in the first place. "I'm here because of my experience and knowledge," they think. "That's what makes me executive material." Believing this is their primary value to the company, they act accordingly, bold and confident even in the face of a lack of data.

A leader's true value to the company, however, comes from the fact that they are able to process the right data. The biggest problem isn't a lack of experience or confidence, it's a lack of data. They are missing a vital piece of information that would enable them to become a rock star decision-maker who blasts out of the starting gate headed in exactly the right direction.

To put it another way, it's like driving to a scheduled meeting at a certain location in a city where you know the roads fairly well. You choose the best route based on your knowledge of the layout of the city streets, but you lack information about current traffic conditions. Consequently, you go a few blocks, turn a corner at a familiar intersection, and find yourself stuck in traffic due to an unforeseen accident up ahead.

If you'd just checked the Waze app on your phone, you would have seen the accident in advance, so you could have planned a more effective route. You would also have seen places where traffic is slowed due to construction, the location of speed traps, possibly a funeral or special event taking place somewhere. This was data you needed to ensure you arrived at your destination in time.

Instead, you just drove off relying on your biases with no way to know for sure if you could make it. With the right data, you could have rerouted, taken a different approach, and avoided a lot of unexpected anxiety and possibly a missed appointment.

In essence, that's what companies are dealing with—leaders who won't take the time up front to measure—and it's killing them. It's ruining careers and destroying company growth. It's preventing the realization of so many amazing ideas.

THE SOLUTION

Leaders have to stop talking about strategy and innovation as if it's the problem.

The problem in your company's growth may not be your strategy or ability to innovate, and it might have nothing to do with economics at all. It might simply be your company's ability to execute on initiatives. What's the solution?

Measuring your company's readiness and capability to implement each project has a direct consequence on ROIC, the key driver of value. Doing it on an annual basis isn't enough. There are too many variables and changing conditions. The data indicates it must be measured for every individual initiative on its own merits. Every initiative is unique, and your company's execution capability will vary from initiative to initiative. That sounds exhausting, but it doesn't have to be.

Measuring execution capability gives you the ability to make better decisions, but it also collects data on a continuous basis, which helps you understand the overall health of your business, as well as its ability to adapt to the future. No longer will you have to operate on assumption. Instead, you'll come flying out of the gate pointed in the right direction, knowing that you have the ability to win the race.

CHAPTER 2

BIAS IN DECISION-MAKING

Mark Olander is the CEO of TaxAudit, the audit provider for QuickBooks by Intuit, so any time an Intuit customer does their taxes, they have the option to purchase audit coverage for their tax return. TaxAudit handles audit investigations each year on behalf of Intuit customers that have bought their coverage. They use a digital platform, and not long ago, they were looking for a way to modernize that platform in order to increase their automation and ability to process a higher volume.

Mark understood he had one shot to get it right, or his business and reputation would suffer.

Not only would this change require a significant financial investment in the restructuring of their product platform, but it would require numerous changes to their workflow. This would require changing the way they managed the company internally, as they opened new offices and hired new people in multiple locations to meet the demand for the increase in the volume of work.

In essence, it was a significant step up for their business, and Mark wanted to understand what their chances were for successfully implementing the required changes. He was concerned about the decision-making process because he didn't know what he didn't know. To eliminate this uncertainty, he chose to measure his execution capability so he could eliminate any impediments to their strategy.

Upon investigating their execution capability, Mark discovered that his executive team had numerous biases in their decision-making. Specifically, they had applied assumptions in what they believed their teams could accomplish and how many of their staff could fully participate in the implementation. When they looked past these biases, they realized there were roadblocks that could potentially hinder their strategy. Some of them were things they had suspected but couldn't articulate and hadn't been able to verify with data. Others were a complete surprise.

By measuring their execution capability, they revealed specific vulnerabilities, which forced them to reexamine their approach. In the end, they restructured their entire strategy. As a result, they wound up being able to eliminate the vulnerabilities, and they were able to execute their transformational change on time. They weren't investing money in initiatives that weren't producing results or that went well beyond the timeframe they had anticipated.

By spending a little extra time up front estimating their execution capability, they were able to stay on target and manage the cost model of modernizing their platform. They were then able to manage the higher volume that came with the platform change and deal with the issues that came with growth.

Identifying the vulnerabilities in the beginning led to a more focused and precise execution of strategy, because they didn't trip over those vulnerabilities.

Finally, their successful implementation of their platform change resulted in a stronger and better relationship with Intuit.

CEO Mark Olander and his executive team now swear by the results that an execution capability metric provides. They believe wholeheartedly that they were able to meet their targets while avoiding wasted resources and time because they understood clearly what they were getting into.

FLAWED DECISION-MAKING

If an execution capability metric is so clearly beneficial to implementing a strategy, why don't more executives do it? What is the flaw in their decision-making that encourages them to avoid this vital step?

As it turns out, it's the result of the way operations are structured, especially in Fortune 500 companies. Leaders invest heavily in human capital, process management, and technology. Since they've invested so much money in these things, they assume their people, processes, and technology will be able to adapt to the changing needs brought about by their strategy as they move forward.

The problem is that executive roles, with a few exceptions—notably CEO and CFO—are largely outward-facing. In other words, they are designed to meet milestones and goals for investors. They have public reporting needs that must be met, so they assume that their operations will adapt to future demand.

"If we pour enough money into operations to hire some extra talent, they will adapt to whatever our changing needs happen to be." That's a common way of thinking, and it's a bias that sets them up for disappointment. They fill the gap in their data with this assumption, so they can begin moving forward on strategy.

They might also use past experience to bolster the assumption. "This strategy produced good results in the past, so we predict it will produce good results again." In reality, there is no correlation between past results and future results. It's a false positive that contributes to flawed decision-making.

It's the same thinking that plagued Major League Baseball, as shown in the movie *Moneyball*. Team managers were paying huge money to bring in big-name players. Their biased decision-making told them, "This guy is a huge talent, and we've spent a lot of money on him. He will adapt to whatever the upcoming season throws at us. Plus, he's won a few championships in the past, so surely he will win again." However, they often wound up wringing their hands as a disappointing season unfolded.

In the movie, there's a pivotal scene where Billy Beane, general manager of the Oakland Athletics, has a conversation in a parking garage with Yale economics graduate Peter Brand. Brand points out, "People who run ball clubs, they think in terms of buying players. Your goal shouldn't be to buy players, your goal should be to buy wins."[11]

Baseball scouts were selecting players based on their own personal experience and intuition. Brand suggested that clubs look past their own biases and rely on an actual analysis of performance statistics, particularly "on-base percentage."

WHAT THE RESEARCH REVEALS

The experience of these companies, and their frustrated executives, mirrors much of the research around

---

11   "Moneyball Quotes," IMDb, https://www.imdb.com/title/tt1210166/quotes.

decision bias that has come out in the last twenty years. As it turns out, leaders are just not good at predicting the execution capability of their own companies without hard data, even leaders with years of experience and in-depth knowledge.

According to a study by Daniel Kahneman, Eugene Higgins Professor of Psychology Emeritus at Princeton University, executives regularly make different decisions using the exact same data. Winner of the Nobel Prize in Economic Sciences in 2002, he has done a lot of research on cognitive biases.

Academic researchers have repeatedly confirmed that professionals often contradict their own prior judgments when given the same data on different occasions. For instance, when software developers were asked on two separate days to estimate the completion time for a given task, the hours they projected differed by 71%, on average. When pathologists made two assessments of the severity of biopsy results, the correlation between their ratings was only .61 (out of a perfect 1.0), indicating that they made inconsistent diagnoses quite frequently. Judgments made by different people are even more likely to diverge. Research has confirmed that in many tasks, experts' decisions are highly variable: valuing stocks, appraising real estate, sentencing criminals, evaluating job performance, auditing financial statements, and more.[12]

Despite this, the study also pointed out that experienced professionals tend to have a high confidence in the accuracy of their own judgments and a high regard for colleague intelligence. The end result, according to Kahneman, is that "professionals often make decisions that deviate significantly from those of their peers, from their own prior decisions, and from rules that they themselves claim to follow." His conclusion: "As a rule, we believe that neither professionals nor their managers can make a good guess about the reliability of their judgments."

In a speech at the 71st CFA Institute Annual Conference in Hong Kong, Kahneman warned that executives are setting themselves up for frustration by only studying the success stories. "Overconfidence is a curse," he said, later adding, "If you look at everyone, there is lots of failure...We trust our intuitions even when

---

12 Daniel Kahneman, Andrew M. Rosenfield, Linnea Gandhi, Tom Blaser, "Noise: How to Overcome the High, Hidden Cost of Inconsistent Decision Making," *Harvard Business Review, October* 2016, https://hbr.org/2016/10/noise.

they're wrong." He went on to point out that "research demonstrates that experience increases the confidence with which people hold their ideas, but not necessarily the accuracy of those ideas." Noting the danger of such confidence, he added, "When somebody tells you that they have a strong hunch about a financial event, the safe thing to do is not to believe them."[13]

American economist Richard Thaler published similar findings. As an article on his research in *Quartz* explained, "We like to believe that we are smart, rational creatures, always acting in our best interests. In fact, dominant economic theory these days often makes that assumption. What was left of this illusion was further dismantled by The Royal Swedish Academy of Sciences, who awarded the Nobel prize in economics to Richard Thaler, an American economist at the University of Chicago, for his pioneering work in behavioral economics, which examines humanity's flaws—namely, why we don't make rational economic decisions."[14]

---

13 Paul McCaffrey, "Daniel Kahneman: Four Keys to Better Decision Making," *Enterprising Investor, June* 8, 2018, https://blogs. cfainstitute.org/investor/2018/06/08/daniel-kahneman-four-keys-to-better-decision-making/.

14 Eshe Nelson, "The flaws a Nobel Prize-winning economist wants you to know about yourself," *Quartz, October* 9, 2017, https://qz.com/1098078/behavioral-economics-the-flaws-that-economics-nobel-prize-winner-richard-thaler-wants-you-to-know-about-yourself/.

Thaler's conclusion is that humans do not act entirely rationally when it comes to decision-making. Specifically, they are influenced by social preferences and a lack of self-control in the decision process.[15] In *Nudge: Improving Decisions About Health, Wealth, and Happiness*, a book he co-wrote with Harvard professor Cass Sunstein, he puts it bluntly: "People often make poor choices—and look back at them with bafflement! We do this because as human beings, we all are susceptible to a wide array of routine biases that can lead to an equally wide array of embarrassing blunders in education, personal finance, health care, mortgages and credit cards, happiness, and even the planet itself."[16]

Researchers Donald Sull, Rebecca Homkes, and Charles Sull conducted a survey of 7,600 managers in 262 companies across thirty different industries, focusing specifically on strategy execution. Their conclusion:

"Several widely held beliefs about how to implement strategy are just plain wrong."

---

15 Professor Richard Thaler, "Why Richard Thaler won the 2017 economics Nobel Prize," *The Conversation, October* 9, 2017, http://theconversation.com/why-richard-thaler-won-the-2017-economics-nobel-prize-85404.

16 Richard H. Thaler, Cass R. Sunstein, *Nudge: Improving Decisions About Health, Wealth, and Happiness, (Penguin Books: New York,* 2008*)*.

In fact, they pointed out that leaders still don't have a good idea of how to translate strategy into results.

Among the problems they identified, most companies don't adapt quickly enough to changing market conditions, and most leaders believe that a failure in execution can be corrected by increasing alignment between activities up and down the chain of command. There's also an unfortunate tendency to invest in nonstrategic projects. As the authors said rather pointedly, "It's pretty dire when half the C-suite cannot connect the dots between strategic priorities."

They concluded:

In the worst cases, companies slip into a dynamic we call the alignment trap. When execution stalls, managers respond by tightening the screws on alignment— tracking more performance metrics, for example, or demanding more frequent meetings to monitor progress and recommend what to do. This kind of top-down scrutiny often deteriorates into micromanagement, which stifles the experimentation required for agility and the peer-to-peer interactions that drive coordination. If managers focus too narrowly on improving alignment, they risk developing ever more refined answers to the wrong question. Seeing execution suffer but not knowing why, managers turn once more to the tool they know best and further tighten alignment. The end result: Companies are trapped in a downward spiral in which more alignment leads to worse results. [17]

Even CEOs are struggling. The authors pointed to a recent survey of 400 CEOs in companies around the world which "found that executional excellence was the number one challenge facing corporate leaders in Asia, Europe, and the United States, heading a list of some 80 issues, including innovation, geopolitical instability, and top-line growth." The authors added, "We also know that execution is difficult. Studies have found that two-thirds to three-quarters of large organizations struggle to implement their strategies."

Management consulting firm McKinsey conducted a global survey of executives in which they attempted to "assess the frequency and intensity of the most common managerial biases in companies." They identified the problem as follows: "It's clear that the vagaries of

---

17 Donald Sull, Rebecca Homkes, Charles Sull, "Why Strategy Execution Unravels—and What to Do About It," *Harvard Business Review, March* 2015, https://hbr.org/2015/03/why-strategy-execution-unravelsand-what-to-do-about-it.

individual and group psychology can cause irrational decision making by both individuals and organizations, resulting in less than ideal outcomes."

In their study, they asked executives a series of questions about a single recent strategic decision that had either a satisfactory or unsatisfactory outcome, focusing particularly on the role biases played in the decision-making process. Their conclusion reinforced many of the ideas we're discussing in this book.

"It's evident from the results that satisfactory outcomes are associated with less bias, thanks to robust debate, an objective assessment of facts, and a realistic assessment of corporate capabilities...Also notable is that companies that typically make good decisions focus more on their own ability to execute than other companies do."[18]

Companies that typically make good decisions focus more on their own ability to execute than other companies do.

---

18 McKinsey & Company, January 2009, "Flaws in strategic decision making: McKinsey Global Survey results," https://www.mckinsey.com/business-functions/strategy-and-corporate-finance/our-insights/flaws-in-strategic-decision-making-mckinsey-global-survey-results.

Finally, Thomas Redman, Ph.D., in an article in *Harvard Business Review*, warned that many of our failed initiatives are the result of "rigged decisions," which he said unfold like this:

1. You make a decision based on some or all of the following: ego, ideology, experience, fear, or consultation with like-minded advisers.
2. You find data that justifies your decision.
3. You announce and execute the decision, and defend it to the minimum degree necessary.
4. You take credit if the decision proves beneficial, and assign blame if not.

Redman warned against making a decision first and finding data to back it up later. "Faster is not the same as well-thought-out," he said. In today's fast-paced market, however, the temptation to make fast decisions is stronger than ever. As Redman pointed out, "Few people set out to make a rigged decision, but when you're pressured to make a choice fast, you may fall victim to a flawed process."[19]

---

19 Thomas C. Redman, "Root Out Bias from Your Decision-Making Process," *Harvard Business Review*, March 10, 2017, https://hbr.org/2017/03/root-out-bias-from-your-decision-making-process.

Donald Sull, in his article for *MIT Sloan Management Review*, wrote, "Managers can rarely identify all the factors that will end up mattering in the future, let alone predict how events will unfold." In the presence of so much uncertainty, they often "accept the presence of uncertainty, make a best guess on a strategy based on the data at hand, commit to the strategy, and then hope for the best. But even though executives might try to mitigate risk by, for example, diversifying their lines of business, the fundamental logic remains: Place your bets and take your chances."[20]

All of this research seems to paint a bleak picture of the executive decision-making process. Certainly, the frustration caused by the failure of great ideas and poorly implemented strategic initiatives is widespread.

YESTERDAY IS NOT TODAY

As we developed this execution capability metric, we saw the insights of all of this research at play in many different companies, including some of the largest corporations in the world. Leaders are struggling with

---

20 Donald N. Sull, "Closing the Gap Between Strategy and Execution," *MIT Sloan*, July 01, 2007, https://sloanreview.mit.edu/article/closing-the-gap-between-strategy-and-execution/.

strategic implementation at all levels. The confusion is widespread and shows no sign of abating.

Within the largest organizations, the pace of change is now so fast that upper management feels compelled to make fast decisions in order to meet demand, so they substitute data with assumptions to fill in the gaps. Rather than saying, "Our data indicates we can successfully move forward on this initiative," they say, "We've done something similar to this in the past, so let's assume it will work."

These assumptions create a false sense of confidence, but they also allow leaders to implement decisions swiftly. In many instances, politics or other social influences bolster this uninformed decision-making. Some executives, those with high emotional intelligence, are able to "sell" their ideas despite the lack of data, influencing people to approve the initiatives they want to move forward on.

By the time the company decides to implement a strategy, they don't even recognize the mishmash of biases that is informing the decision. They simply assume they are acting as leaders. "This is what we do. We are leaders, so we bring insight and experience and make decisions."

What leaders overlook is that every decision they make has a unique set of conditions that determines whether or not the business can implement it. This is why basing a decision on past success is never a reliable metric. One effort can go incredibly well and then another very similar effort, which might run parallel to the first, overlap it, or occur in sequence, goes horribly wrong.

Once that happens, leaders examine the failure and try to figure out what they did wrong from a process perspective or a Six Sigma perspective or some other perspective, little realizing that the second initiative failed simply because the conditions for each decision are different, even if they happen in sequence.

Delivery teams, product teams, merger and acquisition teams, market growth teams, and back-office teams are only polishing the stone they've been handed. They can't make diamonds out of dust. If you give them good raw materials, they will produce a good outcome. That's what they are trained to do and skilled at doing. That's why you've hired, retained, and continue to invest in them.

Often, teams are expected to *find a way*, but the problem has to do with the conditions. No matter how talented and experienced they are, they can't produce the outcome leaders want in the timeframe they want at the cost level they demand. When they try anyway and fail, leaders say, "What went wrong? Let's go back and analyze the strategy so we can improve our processes."

The fate of the initiative was already determined at the decision point. The team never had the ability to execute it successfully, no matter how many encouragements or corrective meetings they received from management.

As a leader, when you engage a team—whether a product team, marketing team, or acquisition team—the conditions they have to address in order to bring your idea to completion are unique to the business and market for that specific time period. This variability is unavoidable.

Leaders perceive an overarching company health metric that is traditionally company wide and often generally states, "Our business is in good shape. Our project management office is in good shape. We have great developers and engineers, and a skilled analyst. We should be able to implement any strategy." However, the overarching health of the company gives no indication if your teams are ready and able to implement a specific strategy within its specific conditions. It also falls short in taking into consideration any biases that have been introduced into the decision-making process.

Consequently, ideas and strategies that have no chance of success whatsoever get pushed into people, processes, and technologies that are optimized to current conditions. When they fail, leaders point the finger at those very people, processes, and technology, blaming them for a lack of proper execution, little realizing that their teams were attempting to build and fly the plane at the same time. They had no chance of achieving the acquired result, no matter how hard they worked, but this impending doom was obscured behind a curtain of bias and assumption on the part of decision makers.

If only there had been a proper metric on the front end to remove these biases and assumptions. Then leaders could recognize that while the idea was great, there were simply too many obstacles to execute it within the desired cost and timeframe that they'd chosen. This would have spared their teams from a black swan effort that became all-consuming and only achieved half the value or just got killed altogether.

Instead, in the aftermath of the failed initiative, leaders turn inward, looking to root out perceived underperformance. However, conditions simply didn't exist to make success possible, their focus is misplaced.

DANGEROUS TYPES OF BIAS

Though bias can come in many forms, there are eight biases in particular that tend to affect executive decision-making the most. Let's take a look at each of them and reveal how they influence the decision process.

 **Confirmation Bias:** Confirmation bias means seeking and prioritizing information that confirms your existing beliefs. In other words, you're not using the data to inform your decision-making. You're using it selectively to justify what you already believe. We do this in our personal lives all the time. For example, if you're considering going to a specific restaurant, you might do research on Google and Yelp to see what other diners have said about it. However, as you read posted reviews, you begin mentally eliminating the ones that don't support the conclusion you've already come to. "This review is very negative, but I think this person is just bitter. I refuse to take them seriously." We all do this, and we do it constantly—eliminating data that contradicts existing beliefs.

 **Framing Bias:** Framing is when you draw different conclusions from the same information presented differently. This happens frequently in the finance phase, because you can build a pro forma spreadsheet in three different ways, painting very different pictures. Essentially, you are introducing biases and injecting them into the finance model in an attempt to influence how the outcome looks.

 Anchoring Bias: Anchoring refers to excessively focusing on the first piece of information you receive when making a decision. Gossip works this way. The first piece of gossip you hear about a person or situation determines your perception of that person or situation, even when you hear conflicting gossip later on. Donald Sull, in his article for *MIT Sloan Management Review* says, "Research on effective decision-making has found that groups in rapidly changing markets do best to avoid anchoring too quickly on a single view. In novel situations, the best interpretation is rarely obvious, and the obvious one is often wrong."[21]

---

21 Ibid.

 **Sunk Cost Bias:** Sunk cost is the refusal to abandon something that is underperforming or unrewarding simply because you've already invested in it. This happens when leaders say, "We're so far into this strategy, and we've put so many resources into it, we might as well keep going. We can't turn back now. We have to make it work."

 Monte Carlo Bias: Named after the famed gambling destination, Monte Carlo bias means putting excessive weight on previous events, believing that they somehow represent future outcomes. This is more common with older leaders. It's the assumption that past performance dictates future results. "I've seen this before, so I know exactly how it will turn out."

 **Self-Assessment Bias:** Unskilled individuals sometimes overestimate their abilities and experts sometimes underestimate theirs. Highly skilled and knowledgeable people tend to be the most skeptical about the odds of success, while unskilled (often younger) people who lack experience are more likely to say, "Oh, yeah, we got this. We can do it," and then get themselves way in over their heads.

 **Availability Bias:** This refers to over-estimating the importance of information that is easiest to recall. In other words, it's taking whatever is right in front of you as gospel truth. "This is the first thing I got off Google. It must be accurate." Have you ever done a Google search and accepted the accuracy of the top search result? Have you ever had a stack of documents, read the first one, and accepted its conclusion? These are examples of availability bias.

 Bandwagon Bias: When we jump on the bandwagon, it means we believe or do something simply because the people around us are doing it. We say, "This is what everyone else is doing, so I guess it's the thing to do. They must be right."

This is by no means an exhaustive list. There are many forms of decision bias. Studies have shown that humans make 95 percent of their decisions using mental short-cuts or rules of thumbs.[22] That's where many of these biases come into play, and when we allow any of them to

22 Sarah Moss-Horwitz, "Designing for Better Decision Making," *Medium*, Nov 18, 2017, https://medium.com/behaveux/designing-for-better-decision-making-86d9f40ff003.

influence our thinking, they get us pointed in the wrong direction right out of the gate. They skew the prospective decision makers on what should happen, and it's only when the implementation starts to go wrong that the truth behind the biases is revealed—and the truth can be harsh and unforgiving.

Unfortunately, by the time the biases and assumptions start to break down, you're in the throes of delivering on an initiative that has a schedule aligned to a budget. You've already made your forecast and set a project schedule, and the desperation begins to mount as it becomes clear just how difficult, even impossible, it's going to be to meet it. Now, all of those vulnerabilities that you overlooked or failed to uncover begin percolating and rising to the surface.

When that happens, effort is diverted to damage control, even as the initiative falls farther and farther behind. All because leaders had limited information, market research was off, cultural alignment wasn't quite right, or the decision-making team had competing priorities. There are so many factors that can be glossed over because leaders say, "Our processes will handle it. Our people will figure it out. That's what they do. They adapt and deal with problems."

Even if they are able to overcome unexpected problems, it might take your team months to find and implement a solution, throwing you way off your timeframe. Not only do you have to invest extra money to fund the fix, but you now have to spend more money to make up for lost time. It's like the runner who started the race pointed three degrees in the wrong direction. When they finally realized they'd veered way off track, they first had to get reoriented in the right direction and then they had to run twice as hard to make up the extra distance. All of this compounds, one consequence feeding another, until it becomes absolutely hopeless.

WHAT'S THE ANSWER?

How can you avoid finding yourself in this terrible death spiral during the implementation of your next strategic initiative? The answer is simple: fill in the gap with data instead of bias. You need a true measurement of your execution capability for every initiative associated with an overall strategy.

This isn't a once-a-year measurement, nor a mere general assessment of the health of your business. It's not a once-a-month analysis of a specific business unit. Rather, you are measuring each individual initiative on its own, because each initiative is influenced by factors independent of any other initiative.

Don't assume there's predictability in your delivery capability. For example, if you own a lawn care service, your ability to deliver top-notch services on a sunny day will vary widely from your ability to deliver on a rainy day, even though the same people and equipment are being used each time. If you make tables for a living, the quality of the wood you use for each table will vary. This variable demands individual capability measurements for each initiative, no matter your product, service, or industry.

People try so hard to control environmental conditions or process conditions when they should be considering how vulnerabilities will impact the delivery process so they can address those vulnerabilities prior to implementation. When you clear the vulnerabilities out of the way, you not only make success achievable but you accelerate your delivery.

As McKinsey's global survey on strategic decision-making concludes, "One of the most frequent practices at companies that make good decisions is the accurate assessment of execution capabilities, indicating that managers should increase their focus on this element when considering strategic options."[23]

Measuring execution capability helps you do that. Let's take a closer look at how it works.

---

23 "Flaws in strategic decision making: McKinsey Global Survey results," *McKinsey & Company*, January 2009, https://www. mckinsey.com/business-functions/strategy-and-corporate-finance/our-insights/flaws-in-strategic-decision-making-mckinsey-global-survey-results.

CHAPTER 3

MEASURE TO WIN

This model was developed over an eight-year period to help leaders figure out what was derailing their efforts to release products on time, move into new markets, acquire companies, and implement back-office modernization to increase efficiencies. Combining our own research with information gleaned from studies out of Ohio State, MIT, Sloan, Princeton, and research published by McKinsey and *Harvard Business Review* (some of which we mentioned earlier), we investigated the root cause of execution capability for individual initiatives and projects.

We observed that much decision-making was the result of financial analysis married to opinions, and this unholy marriage was the root cause of the high failure rate in strategy implementation. What we soon realized is that leaders need a score, some specific measure they can use to determine if they can implement an initiative before they get into the project death spiral.

The execution capability score is intended to identify if a company is able to execute on a specific idea. If the answer is marginal to yes, then they know what vulnerabilities to address before engaging the delivery process. If the answer is marginal to no, regardless of the value of the idea, then leaders know they have to let it go because it will consume the company and won't produce any value to the bottom line.

DOMAINS OF MEASUREMENT

In the process of developing this metric, we identified fourteen domains of measurement that allow for the calculation of a single number. Then we identified the specific vulnerabilities associated with each of those fourteen domains, so company leaders can identify the source of a low score and take corrective action.

By measuring your execution capability for every initiative, you accelerate the implementation by clarifying your direction and clearing the road ahead of obstacles. As a result, you get your desired result for a lower cost on delivery and a significantly higher return on investment.

After all, if 50 percent of what you're doing is a waste, you are negatively impacting ROIC and earnings per share (EPS). If you can end that erosion, you can reclaim and redirect those lost funds in a more fruitful direction. This metric gives you that opportunity. If you have a set amount of dollars on the table, it allows you to understand exactly which initiatives will generate the best return for your business.

WHAT'S THE PRECEDENT?

Of course, there's precedent for using a single score as the basis for decision-making. We see this in many industries. Universities use SAT and ACT scores in college admissions. Lenders use FICO Scores to determine credit risk. Bond ratings are used to indicate the credit quality of a bond to a potential investor. Personality test scores are used in hiring as part of the overall assessment of a potential new hire.

Types of Execution Capability Scoring

Lending	Application	+ Financials	+ FICO Score = Yes/No
Higher Education	Application	+ Transcript	+ SAT/ACT Score = Yes/No
Bonds	Financing Plan +	Offering Documents +	Bond Rating = Yes/No
Hiring	Resume	+ Interview	+ Personality Profiled = Yes/No

In fact, execution capability has been measured in various ways for at least a hundred years in numerous industries, but for some reason, executive decision-making has been the exception. The corporate world remains practically medieval. With the increasing pace of operations and expectations, the consequences of a bad decision come fast and hard. Often, companies only get one shot. There's just not enough time for serious course correction.

Just as a credit score can immediately reveal a major credit risk, an execution capability score immediately identifies an initiative that just won't work for you. Of course, you might be thinking, "Yes, but credit score, SAT and ACT scores, and bond rating all get skewed to some degree, don't they?"

Possibly, but at the end of the day, each of those scores must be backed by measurable data, and that data provides a critical piece of information to inform decisions moving forward. At the very least, they give key decision makers a more objective look at specific options.

In the case of credit score, a bank or venture capital firm is trying to decide whether or not to invest in someone, and the credit score provides an easy way to determine if that person has a track record of repaying investments. Originally developed by Fair, Isaac, and Company, the credit score was intended to help identify possible credit risks.

With the passage of the Fair Credit Reporting Act in 1970, credit reporting bureaus began publishing their data, but lenders struggled to compare and interpret reports from multiple agencies. They lacked a single, unified metric. The credit score was intended to fill this gap, using an algorithm that measured a variety of relevant factors and provided lenders with an easy-to-understand score.

If you went to a lender today and said, "I want to buy this nice house over here," they would check your credit score because that number gives them some indication of your ability to repay the loan. If your credit score comes back as a measly 520, they almost certainly won't give you a loan, even if they have yet to look at your actual financials. Even if you can prove you have a decent job with a respectable income, your credit score reveals a possible deeper problem that might otherwise show up later as missed mortgage payments or even a defaulted loan.

In the case of SAT and ACT scores, a single number from a standardized test provides a clear sense of whether or not an applicant has the education and intelligence to succeed at a specific university. After all, prestigious universities have to comb through thousands of applications, looking for the cream of the crop, which might be 5 percent or less of total applicants.

Before the SAT was introduced in 1926, universities typically had their own admissions tests, and some admitted students based solely on their high school grades. At the turn of the twentieth century, an organization known as the College Board began offering entrance exams, but they were designed to test *received knowledge* rather than aptitude for learning.

Much like execution capability, a student's aptitude for learning was really the determining factor in their success or failure at college. Princeton psychology professor Carl Brigham developed SAT to fill the gap in data, testing a student's *ability* to learn, rather than merely assessing what they had already learned.[24]

With a bond rating, a municipality's ability to repay its debt becomes clear. Municipalities that perform very well have a higher bond rating, so they are able to get money at a lower rate of return to the investor. Those with a lower rating have a higher rate of return because they create a higher risk for the investor.

Personality tests are another example of using a single score for decision-making, which is why so many organizations today use them during the hiring process. With a single score, a personality test can reveal if an applicant is a good or bad culture fit, providing information that otherwise might not be gleaned from the job interview and employment history alone.

In a similar way, corporate decision makers need a single score that can provide key guidance for strategic decision-making by removing bias and assumption.

---

24 "The History of the SAT," *Manhattan Review,* https://www. manhattanreview.com/sat-history/.

EXECUTION CAPABILITY FUELS THE DECISION ENGINE

The purpose of an execution capability score is about taking a list of initiatives and being able to rank them. Which ones are good ideas, have strong financial forecasts, and, just as importantly, which ones do you have the ability to execute? With this metric, you can push those initiatives to the top of the list and relegate biased initiatives to the rubbish bin.

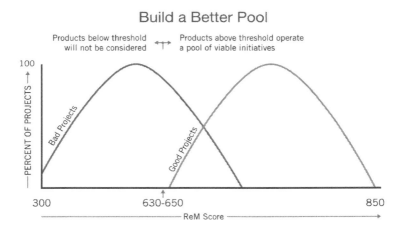

Fundamentally, you're building a better pool of initiatives. By showing you which ones are lost causes, you can take those off the table, leaving only those your company has the ability to successfully implement within your desired timeframe and budget. From that better list, you can now have a real discussion about what strategy you want to pursue.

With that better pool of initiatives, you can begin applying other filters: Is it a strong business case? Does the outcome support the direction we want to go as a business? Do the financials look good?

As a result, you can make faster decisions with greater precision. You can articulate the value of an initiative with greater accuracy, and the people who are the next level down in your organization—or two levels down, or five—can trust that the yes-or-no decision was based on data rather than some executive's hunch, assumption, or personal preference.

The people who now have to execute that initiative can do so with more faith and confidence, so getting complete "buy-in" at every level of the organization is easier. People begin to trust executive decision-making, which gives them greater confidence in the direction of the company. No longer will they look at every executive decision through a skeptical lens.

Bear in mind, in most organizations, employees view executive decision-making as fairly haphazard, even random. The value of executives as a whole is under a constant light of judgment, so people tend to approach every decision with caution and even cynicism.

Now that decisions are backed by data, employees feel more confident that initiatives are "doable." Executives, in turn, know they are earning the trust of their organization. By eliminating bias, executives can apply their experience and knowledge in a more effective way, optimizing every part of the business, so they start to realize better outcomes, which also feeds ROIC and investor confidence.

At the same time, because executives have a better pool of initiatives to choose from, they can communicate them better externally. Now, they can approach the investors and analysts and speak with confidence about their strategy because they don't have to dance around the assumptions and bias that went into the decision-making process.

No longer will you create situations where you have a great idea, your people pour a lot of energy into it, and then four or five months later, they start to see erosion. No longer will they feel the mounting frustration of working harder and harder but falling farther and farther behind, as they begin to think, "How in the world are we going to make this work?"

Instead, you've created a decision engine that is precise and efficient, and since it's connected throughout the business, people at every level begin to believe in the company, in the wisdom of leadership, and in the possibility of achieving the desired outcome.

PART TWO

MEASURING EXECUTION CAPABILITY

CHAPTER 4

MEASURING WHAT MATTERS

Before they decided to measure execution capability, TaxAudit began investing in hiring for their project team in an effort to ramp up the capacity to handle the impending increase in volume. They believed that if they could build a more robust project management office, it would make the difference moving forward, ensuring success in the modernization of their core product platform.

They aren't alone in this approach. In fact, this tends to be the approach most companies take when preparing for some big initiative: they invest in hiring more people. If it's a technology project, they go out and hire more technology people and buy new software. This seems to make sense. It's logical, right?

Except that's often not where the real vulnerabilities lie. As in the case of TaxAudit, the vulnerabilities are more often a result of executives not having a clear sense of what the business is capable of doing. Rather than simply hiring more people to handle more volume, they needed to take a holistic look at their capabilities to discover the things that would impair execution.

The idea of modernizing their core platform was the right initiative, but they were unclear about the capability of their operations to support the initiative. In the end, they had to take a step back, retrench, and take a look at the role operations played in the overall strategy. What they needed was clear data, not merely a sense of what they were capable of implementing.

Measuring execution capability boils down to taking a look at the areas of your company that will impact an initiative. You're doing more than gathering documents or merely looking at the execution of previous initiatives. You're looking far more broadly at the whole gamut of domains that will affect the execution.

Once TaxAudit did this, they began to identify and correct their real vulnerabilities. However, despite their eventual success, when they first measured execution capability, they wrestled to apply all of the data it provided. They had put such weight into their biases that some of the indicators from execution capability measurement seemed counterintuitive. They couldn't understand how it would actually affect the outcome of their initiative.

They accepted that the vulnerabilities revealed were valid, but they struggled to prioritize and take all of them seriously. They had to learn how to link the metrics to the downstream effects, because their assumptions and biases about what was critical were so entrenched. It was essentially a two-step process of learning what was truly important and then applying it.

A FRANKENSTEIN OF BEST PRACTICES

Most executives believe they can build a kind of Frankenstein monster of best practices throughout their organization by picking and choosing lessons learned from previous initiatives. Frankenstein's monster was cobbled together from the parts of what he perceived to be the best of different corpses, and the end result was a dangerous and unstable monster.

That's what many executives are creating in the absence of the right execution data. This becomes the static, cookie-cutter approach they use for implementing every initiative, but it doesn't—and can't—account for vulnerabilities that are fluid and unique to each initiative being considered.

Consequently, the team ends up spending much of their time correcting issues that arise from those vulnerabilities while trying, at the same time, to maintain the cookie-cutter approach. Every time the team layers another action on top of the process to keep it moving forward, they add stress to existing vulnerabilities, and the whole thing gets worse.

A process that replaces insight and measurement with assumption and bias simply can't carry the load. Often, a single initiative gets subdivided into two, three, or four separate projects in a futile attempt to make up for the gap in capability. That's when the schedule begins to deteriorate, costs accelerate, and problems compound. The strategy might have a clear line of sight, but the execution becomes a wildly meandering process that dilutes the outcome and desired benefit.

THE CALPERS STORY

California Public Employees' Retirement System (CalPERS) manages pension and health benefits for more than 1.6 million public employees, retirees, and their families. In fact, they manage the largest public pension fund in the nation.

Their board had no tolerance for meandering projects that slipped and slid all over the place. More importantly, since they wanted to modernize their actuarial system, they knew they were dealing with a complex model that would require calculating over 3,200 different pension plans for every labor group in the state of California. Adding to the difficulty, every labor group participating in the pension system approached it from an individual and singular perspective.

Leaders at CalPERS knew their modernization effort had to be precise and on-time because the majority of their forecasting, their ability to meet audits, and their ability to function as a unit all depended on the accuracy and timeliness of the actuarial group. However, they were looking at replacing a twenty-five-year-old system that was highly depended upon, a system that had been developed as a grassroots effort. Somehow, the replacement had to stay on track, because they didn't have much leeway, in terms of time and cost, from the board.

This was the motivating factor in deciding to run an execution capability score. When they did, they realized that some issues within their organization they hadn't considered serious were in fact major potential vulnerabilities in the execution of their initiative. Most significantly, CalPERS realized that the project mostly focused on the actuarial group's core needs and did not directly address impacts to all the other dependent operating units that actively utilize their outcomes and data every day.

In response to their results, they spent nine months correcting the critical vulnerabilities they'd identified. While that might sound like a lot of time, in reality, clearing away the vulnerabilities that would have been significant and costly impediments, provided their highly skilled teams the ability to focus their efforts on a modernization effort that successfully came in ahead of schedule and significantly under budget.

By taking the time up front to measure what was critical in executing the modernization of their actuarial system, they accelerated the implementation of their strategy, while also reducing cost and exposure. It gave them the ability to understand how to move forward in the most efficient way, which provided the project team with a firm foundation for doing the hard work of implementation. They were able to see any obstacles that would impede their process well in advance, so the teams from multiple operating units could work together to avoid tripping on them.

EXECUTION CAPABILITY AS AN ACCELERATOR

There's a saying in the military, "Go slow to go fast." You can no longer afford to jump into the deep end of the pool with both feet. That model simply doesn't work anymore. You must do metric assessment on the front end to determine if you're jumping in the right pool. When you take the time to measure execution capability, you accelerate your ability to execute.

Measuring execution capability isn't merely a twenty-minute, five-question self-assessment. While calculating the score can be completed in a day, making corrections takes far more time. This is typical for a large multi-year project, because it's a deep dive into each of the critical areas in the business that will directly impact a specific initiative within a specific timeframe.

This makes some leaders nervous. Others want to take the measurement lightly, as if to say, "We might as well try it. Let's just toss a little execution capability into the mix and see if it helps." To get the most out of it, you have to take it seriously, because the vulnerabilities you are going to uncover aren't typically on the surface. In other instances, the vulnerabilities aren't perceived as *real* because of existing biases, training, and the old "thinking" of established leadership that says if you just hire better people or more tech, you can make any strategy work.

It's hard for some leaders to accept that execution gets impaired by variables they've either completely missed or underweighted. However, by measuring key impact areas, they are able to understand the corrective actions they need to put in place before execution begins. As they take those corrective actions, they can revisit their score to see if those vulnerabilities have been patched. In the end, those areas of vulnerability can be turned into accelerators.

Once you clear the road for your team, they can focus all of their efforts purely on execution. When that happens, it's amazing how much and how fast they can get things done. No longer are they trying to correct issues in process, seeing compounding costs and schedule impacts that trickle down into morale impacts, which then trickle down into executive frustration, market skepticism, and damaged faith from investors that creates a perception of weakness in the company's ability to thrive in the economy.

What it comes down to is this: you no longer have to rely on a strategy of hope, of crossed fingers and hunches. An execution capability score gives you the data to create a strategy based on reality, and that changes everything.

CHAPTER FIVE

WHY CURRENT DECISION PRACTICES DON'T WORK

During the recession in 2008, the default rate in real estate in the United States was between 18 and 20 percent. Consider the impact that had on investor confidence, even the overall global psyche. A mere 20 percent default rate made people feel like the world was falling apart. The media was filled with horror stories.

Can you imagine what would have happened if the default rate had been 50 percent? It would have led to widespread chaos and panic. Yet that, in a sense, is the default rate in corporate strategy in the United States.

Fifty percent of strategies are failing, which means 50 percent of strategic initiatives that corporations are investing in are generating little or no value to the bottom line. Instead of panicking, leaders just assume that's the cost of doing business. In previous decades, you had time to correct a bad decision, and if you terminated a disappointing initiative, you could retrench and come back to it. The problem today is the market moves too quickly.

Consider that the average product development time has shrunk from eighteen months to about six months, while companies typically make two to three strategic turns per year. Whether you're in the public or private sector, this super-pace in the market means you get one chance. If that one chance doesn't work out according to expectations, you quickly find yourself in damage control mode.

When 50 percent of your initiatives go bad, you create a consistency of failure, so your staff stops believing in the direction of the company. They start putting in 50 percent effort because they know from experience that a lot of their hard work is a waste of time. Many of the initiatives you hand off to them won't work out, and they know it. This is all part of the compounding effect of bad initiatives.

This is why we're seeing such deterioration in the S&P 500, where, as we said earlier, the average life of a company on the S&P 500 has dropped from seventy-five years to a pitiful fifteen years. The old security and consistency have been threatened by the fact that half of the ideas and half of the direction given by corporate executives result in projects that don't work. To survive, you now have to balance your decision-making process with execution capability as much as you balance it with innovation.

Consider, for example, Walmart's fight to compete with Amazon. They spent millions to develop their e-commerce business, but they wound up with a website that is little different than the websites of Target, Costco, or any of their other competitors. They waited too long, and it hasn't worked. As an article in *Business Insider* points out, "Walmart can't afford to falter in its war with Amazon. It's already starting from a few paces behind."[25]

In the 1970s and 80s, the speed of business was roughly 25 percent slower than it is today. At any moment, the

---

25 Dennis Green, "Walmart's online struggles show how far it has to go in its war with Amazon," February 21, 2018, https://www.businessinsider.com/walmart-struggles-in-war-with-amazon-2018-2.

stability of an established company can be rocked by the sudden appearance of an innovative startup. The barrier of entry is so low that a startup can go from being nowhere on the radar to being a major threat practically overnight, and startups have much more nimbleness. They can move fast and generate massive social movement. Before an established company can react, a startup can suddenly be trending, and corporate leaders are caught flat-footed.

These established companies rarely lack innovation. Most of them have creative leaders who love to think outside the box, but they simply can't execute on the innovation fast or effectively enough. It is this lack of execution capability that is eating them at their core.

Let's do some simple math. If you're a billion-dollar company and you spend on average 10 percent of your revenue on strategic initiatives, that's $100 million a year. At a 50 percent failure rate, that means you're spending $50 million on things that generate no value to your bottom line. If you can't meet your topline number, and you're struggling with earnings per share, the bad initiatives are directly impacting your ROIC and ROCE (return on capital employed) and degrading market confidence.

Increasing focus on execution capability can start to chip away at that 50 percent default rate by addressing vulnerabilities and accelerating your strategies. Once you implement initiatives faster and more efficiently, while avoiding the initiatives that are doomed to fail, an acceleration effect of go-to-market strategies can be seen. The initiatives you implement have better execution, increasing ability to meet targets, and adapting your decision engine to match innovation and market demand.

UNLEARNING WHAT YOU HAVE LEARNED

Leaving behind the old decision model requires unlearning much of what have been traditional practices. The focus is transforming the decision process so you can make decisions with increased precision. This will lead to a process that can handle the aggressive pace of the markets and the increased capacity of globalization.

You're no longer just competing against American and European firms anymore. You are operating in a global environment, where you also have to deal with Asian, South American, and African firms that are participating and generating innovation at a frenzied pace.

To compete, stripping out biases is essential. In the past, those decisions were exclusively left to the business case and financials, but now they can be supported by more data—data that can be collected quickly in a metric that is digestible and applicable. You simply don't have time to recover from errors. Your window of opportunity into the market will go away.

Ultimately, you're moving to a management model where leaders are able to articulate to global analysts not only that they have innovative ideas and strategies to bring about the next iteration of the company, but that they are also capable of measuring their ability to execute those strategies, balancing it against the value and cost. When you are able to do that, the value of your management team and their skillset goes up.

Being able to articulate that you are measuring every initiative you're investing in—from strategic acquisitions to new products to new markets to back-office modernization—is one of the intangible qualities analysts look at in a well-run company, and it affects investor confidence greatly.

An execution capability score gives executives the ability to gain insight about the health and positioning of their company to meet current and future strategic needs, which makes a profound difference in the market.

BUILD A HIVE MIND

Everything you need to know exists in your company—you just have to harvest the data. Executives settle on a particular strategy because they are convinced it's the right path for their company, and here's the surprising fact: most of the time, they're correct. It *is* the right path.

What they lack is the insight to understand if they can implement it, so they pass the strategy to their teams and tell them to make it happen. When their teams run into problems, it becomes an exercise in frustration and futility trying to figure out why the strategy isn't working, and that's because problems are encompassed in these fourteen different domains of measurement.

A key component of measuring execution capability is the application of Swarm Intelligence (or a "hive mind"), which was developed in 1989 by Jing Wang for cellular robotic systems. This entails applying a Swarm platform (such as ReM Score™) as a network of distributed users who are organized into "human swarms" through a real-time closed-loop model. As revealed by Rosenberg, such real-time systems enable groups of human participants to behave as a unified collective intelligence that works as a single entity to make predictions, answer questions, and evoke opinions.[26]

Such systems, also referred to as "Artificial Swarm Intelligence" (or the brand name Swarm AI) have been shown to significantly amplify human intelligence, resulting in a string of high-profile predictions of extreme accuracy. Academic testing reveals that human swarms can out-predict individuals across a variety of real-world projections. Famously, human swarming was used to correctly predict the Kentucky Derby Superfecta, against 541-to-1 odds, in response to a challenge from reporters.[27]

The hive-mind-based execution capability metric that is outlined in this book relies on fourteen key domains

---

26 Louis B. Rosenberg, "Human Swarms, a real-time paradigm for Collective Intelligence," *Unanimous A.I, San Francisco, California,* 2015.

27 Anthony Cuthbertson, "Artificial Intelligence Turns $20 into $11,000 in Kentucky Derby Bet," *Newsweek, May* 10, 2016, https://www.newsweek.com/artificial-intelligence-turns-20-11000-kentucky-derby-bet-457783.

on a continuous basis. By leveraging an internal "hive network" within your business, you can leverage a unified dynamic system that can quickly assimilate data that converges on the preferred approach. Human swarming uniquely has the ability to harvest a collective intelligence of online groups, which exceeds individual abilities.

By tapping into the collective intelligence resident in your company, the ability to clearly identify which initiatives can be delivered and what vulnerabilities they possess. Next, we'll look at what whose domains are and why they matter.

CHAPTER 6

DOMAINS OF MEASUREMENT

I f you merely take a holistic measurement of your entire business and its ability to execute projects as a one-time measurement, it provides you no relevant data. The conditions under which any particular strategic activity is implemented changes because market conditions change, conditions within the company change, the people participating change, and priorities change.

I keep hammering this point because executives will often receive a one-time evaluation, or examine their previous history, and assume they have an accurate indication of future success. In fact, this actually creates yet another bias that interferes with decision-making.

In a similar way, it's not enough to simply evaluate a single domain. If you're considering an IT project, it's not enough to evaluate your technology capability. If you're deciding on an acquisition, it's not enough to measure your revenue opportunity. If it's a product launch, it's not enough to measure market response.

Executives tend to measure the one domain they think is most relevant to the initiative and assume it gives them the information they need to make an informed decision, but there is a lot more at play in any strategy. In essence, they are applying confirmation bias—a particularly dangerous form of bias in which people prioritize information that confirms their existing beliefs, as we discussed earlier. You have to consider all of the factors that will impact your ability to execute.

EXECUTION CAPABILITY AND SUCCESS

With all we've said about this issue, it's important to remember that execution capability and success are two different things. In other words, measuring execution capability reveals your team's ability to accomplish a strategic initiative during a specific period of time, but it doesn't guarantee that the outcome will be exactly what you wanted. It only reveals whether or not that outcome is *possible*, even *likely*. Your teams still have to work hard to make it happen.

However, what happens in the absence of such a measurement is that decision makers move on strategies in which success was *never* a possibility. There were too many impediments, too many unrevealed vulnerabilities, to achieve the desired outcome. They were doomed to fail from the start and didn't know it.

That's the tragic situation we are eliminating with an execution capability score, giving leaders a grounded look at their ability to execute on a specific initiative. As a result, you make decisions with a broad understanding of all the factors that will impact its implementation. It's about exchanging what you *think* you know for hard, measurable, and applicable data from *all* relevant domains, so you have a balanced equation moving forward.

UNIVERSALLY APPLICABLE DOMAINS

How did we arrive at these fourteen specific domains? As we established a single, baseline metric for decision-making, we used numerous studies and analyses to arrive at the specific domains that have an impact on execution. This information can't be gleaned from a single study. No one has yet produced a single study that looks at all of the domains of measurement impacting executive decision-making, but we were able to access a wide range of research to bring this information together.

Through multiple studies addressing multiple issues, it soon became clear where the key metrics were located for different areas of a company. For example, if you're looking at alignment, there are studies that talk about aligning a business to a strategic initiative. There are other studies that talk about how leadership and governance impact execution.

To develop these domains, we used studies from Princeton, MIT, Ohio State, McKinsey, PWC, hive and swarm intelligence theory, and many others by utilizing key elements of their research to create a single metric touching on fourteen different domains that cover strategic activity. You can read these studies for yourself. Many of them are identified in the appendix of this book and are readily available online.

The fourteen domains we selected are the key indicators that should come into play in decision-making. Bear in mind, each of these domains are universal within their specific area of activity, much like a FICO Score. Your FICO Score doesn't differentiate if you're buying a house, a car, a boat, a business, and so on. It doesn't care if you're a Fortune 500 developer or a kid fresh out of high school.

In the same way, these domains of measurement are universal across all industries and types of initiatives. The fourteen domains are always the same, and the approach is neutral. A potential bias comes into play when leaders believe certain domains only apply to specific types of initiatives. In reality, you might weigh certain domains differently when making your calculation for different initiatives, but the overall information remains the same.

This is because you are measuring the ability to carry out the work—a measurement that applies to every type of initiative. In the case of an acquisition, what you're determining is not only how you're going to integrate the acquisition into your current business financially, culturally, process-wise, and leadership-wise, but also how you're going to sustain that integration going forward.

The successful implementation of an acquisition means the new company will become sustainable and not a liability. All too often, executive leaders acquire a company expecting to add more money to their bottom line, only to discover the hard way that they've overlooked key factors. Soon enough, the acquisition begins dragging the rest of the company down. Measuring execution capability in these key domains prevents this.

THE FOURTEEN DOMAINS OF ReM

With that understanding, let's take a look at the fourteen domains that are measured to determine execution capability. Bear in mind, there are deep layers within each of these domains that we can only touch on at this point, but this will give you a good idea of the significance of each measurement.

ALIGNMENT

Within this single measurement, you are looking at three relevant themes: alignment to strategy, alignment to culture, and alignment to market need. Perhaps you were in a business meeting where a leader announced some great new initiative, and you found yourself scratching your head, wondering, "What does this have to do with where we're trying to go as a business?" Or, "This project is aligned with strategy, but it completely violates our company values. Our culture doesn't work this way. How do we get this ugly duckling to fit in with all of these swans?" Or from a market perspective, "This project is in alignment with our strategy, but the market has no interest in this. If anything, we're years away from the market needing it. We're pulling the trigger too early."

TECHNICAL CAPABILITIES

In today's world, 80 to 90 percent of all strategic initiatives—whether an acquisition, new product launch, or back-office optimization—have a technical component to them, which is vital to the success of the initiative. You simply don't do things on paper anymore. Even construction projects require some technological component—the engineering, the architecture, the calculations, and many other elements. Therefore, you must measure your technical capabilities in any initiative.

MANAGEMENT

You might have a great idea, but do you have people who can lead the initiative? More than someone to sponsor, manage, or take responsibility for the deliverables, you need someone who can actually lead from a structural standpoint.

Do they have the emotional intelligence to lead a team? Do they have the vision and the ability to keep everyone moving together? Many strategic initiatives struggle because they lack good management to make them happen.

TECHNICAL ENVIRONMENT

Are you a cloud-based company, or do you still run your own servers and data warehouses? What technical infrastructure do you have for collecting personal data about people? Can you secure that data? Do you have a means of communicating data security so people believe in your product or service? Does your technical environment have the ability to handle what you're trying to implement?

PRIORITIES

Over time, your priorities might shift, so can the initiative shift along with the changing landscape? Specifically, you will be measuring the financial priority of the initiative, the business need priority, the market priority, and the priority of the executives.

STAKEHOLDERS

Leaders tend to narrow an initiative to the people they believe should be stakeholders, and in the process, they tend to watershed away anyone they believe will be an interference. Even if they don't do this overtly, their biases cause them to favor those who are advocates of the initiative. They avoid anyone who didn't fully support it, even if they don't intend to. As a result, stakeholder influence gets narrower.

When measuring this domain, there's a question that asks users, "Is there anyone else who should be included in this evaluation that you're not seeing on the list?" This gets people thinking. "Oh, maybe Jane should have been included. She might have some key insight." By creating more stakeholders who are investing in the initiative, you deepen your available skills and insight, which can contribute to success.

BUSINESS PROCESS AND RULES MATURITY

In a company or back-office system that is more than five years old, most people tend to understand only the top layer of rules and processes. They lack a deep understanding of those rules and processes, which can become a major hindrance when attempting to implement an initiative.

BUSINESS CAPABILITIES

When you take on a new initiative, you are adding to the workload of a business unit that is probably already at 100 percent functional capacity. Can that business unit handle the new volume of work on top of their regular work? Any strategic initiative is going to be layered on top of an existing full-time job. Do the roles exist internally to handle it, and are there people who understand how to do the work?

You may have a business unit that is well-tuned for the work it's doing today, but with a new initiative, they will have to transform tomorrow. What if the people you need for tomorrow's work don't exist yet inside that business unit? What if your current team lacks the capacity to take on the new work? Even if your existing people tell you they can do the work, they might lack the technical or subject matter knowledge to get it done, and even if they possess the right knowledge, they might lack the bandwidth to take on the extra responsibility.

GOVERNANCE

Do you have a governance process that's well-known by the people participating? Is it well-structured and well-articulated, or is it overly complicated? Does your governance process directly conflict with other processes or operating units? Does it conflict with decision-making processes, culture, or other elements now that you're introducing a governance process that will violate the way certain business units or stakeholder groups work?

If so, you will have to slow down and get those people up to speed within the context of the initiative. Otherwise, people will approach the initiative under their current model and find themselves in conflict with the governance model. That sets any initiative back by six weeks at minimum, because you now have to retrain all of those people.

DECISION-MAKING

Every company, division, and operating unit has a decision-making culture and approach, so the effectiveness of that culture needs to be measured. You need to make sure you have a decision model that complements the initiative. If you have an initiative that needs to move quickly but your operating unit has a decision model that is meticulous and slow-rolling, you're going to run into a problem.

This is one reason why SpaceX has been able to overtake NASA. The decision-making model in NASA is much slower and more cumbersome than the decision-making model at SpaceX, so SpaceX leaders are able to implement their initiatives much faster.

SUBJECT MATTER UNDERSTANDING

How well does your leadership or business understand the subject matter of what they're trying to achieve?

If you're acquiring a company, do you know it well? If you're launching a product, do you have subject matter capability for that product in-house? Because of biases, many people overestimate their understanding of what they're getting into, so this domain provides a clear metric on whether an understanding of the topic already exists or if more research needs to be done.

ORGANIZATIONAL ADAPTABILITY

Depending on the type of business you're in, this domain is where you tend to see a significant bias and impact. If you're trying to move the company from Point A to Point B, it's possible that Point B scares many of your employees because it's changing their jobs, eliminating what they believe to be their job security (such as their existing subject matter knowledge), or exposing them to a new way of doing things (possibly even the dreaded *automation*). Suddenly, they are no longer the expert in the business unit. They're just like everyone else.

The way they do their day-to-day work can feel so disruptive that it becomes an obstacle in realizing that future state. Remember, people don't always resist in an overt way. They don't necessarily protest. Often, their resistance is merely an undercurrent flowing against the intended direction of the initiative. This results in things not getting done in a timely fashion or not getting done with the degree of excellence you hoped for.

If you're acquiring a new company and bringing in new people, processes, and technology, you will see some resistance. Do you know how that clash of cultures is going to impact your ability to move forward?

CRITICALITY

How critical is the initiative in meeting the organization's growth? How critical is it to meeting your intended targets? Sometimes, projects get prioritized over other projects, even though the other projects have a more critical path in the business's viability. Criticality provides a better understanding about how vital a specific initiative is to the overall strategic vision and path of the company.

VISION

Why does Luke Skywalker leave his home planet? Because he wants to become a Jedi. He understands the outcome of his journey, and he can articulate what it will mean. That is the vision that inspires him to make the fateful decision to leave his home planet and begin his adventure. Without a vision, an initiative just becomes an activity you're doing on a daily basis as part of running the company. With a clear vision and the ability to articulate it, you will find it easier to get all participants fully committed and moving in the right direction together.

REVEALING YOUR VULNERABILITIES

Research has shown that these fourteen domains identify critical points at which strategic initiatives fail. By harvesting data on these domains, you reveal your specific vulnerabilities so you can address them before moving forward.

These domains ensure that you take a step back and look more broadly at the things that might hinder your progress. Too often, leaders adopt a narrow view. If they are implementing an IT project, for example, they focus specifically on the company's IT capacity. In most cases, IT is rarely the reason a project doesn't go well. Nine times out of ten, if you stick your IT team in a room with free pizza and access to a toilet, they will knock any IT project out of the park. In reality, if an IT project is having problems, your people are stumbling over issues related to one of these fourteen domains.

Your execution capability is rarely one-dimensional. These fourteen domains are intended to address all of the relevant factors that can trip you up, allowing you to build the plane before you attempt to fly it. Measure these domains one initiative at a time, one project at a time, and address each issue it reveals before moving forward.

You have to constantly harvest the insights from inside your company—not from vendors or consultants or other outside sources. The data exists inside your company, but you have to accumulate that data in an actionable way. By doing so, you reveal the vulnerabilities in each scenario, but you also begin to understand better the operational adaptability of your business.

Once you gather the data and produce this holistic perspective, you can begin to accelerate your strategic process, because you are now able to create a clear path to your desired outcome.

YOU HAVE EVERY ANSWER YOU NEED

Every answer you need regarding what to do, where to go, and how to get there is right inside your company. Executives become so focused on human capital management, trying to resolve every problem by hiring more people, cultivating, and training them, while also relying almost entirely on external consultants and "experts" in strategy or market direction.

However, the answers you seek are already there, just waiting to be harvested. Sadly, companies traditionally listen to consultants and outside influences more than their own people, which is a source of constant frustration for employees.

A fundamental reason we developed the execution capability score is so you can harvest data from your own people. It's that inside data that is consistently overlooked in strategic decision-making and execution. You have all the parts and pieces you need, you just need to put them together in the right way, similar to the way a hive of bees determines the best location for a new nest.

Before measuring execution capability, leaders lacked a clear method of harvesting that data. The participants don't answer direct questions. Instead, they provide answers to indirect questions that enable you to extract relevant information about each of the fourteen domains, enabling the "hive mind" effect to understand capabilities and vulnerabilities. These domains provide a way to extract and harvest the data out of your company, so you can become a strategy execution accelerator.

PART THREE

FINDING YOUR GOLDEN TICKET

CHAPTER 7

BECOMING A STRATEGY EXECUTION ACCELERATOR

A s I've said, the decision-making process is fundamentally broken, stuck in the 1970s and 80s, despite the fact that we're now in an era of super speed. Decision-making in the 1970s wasn't designed to work within today's context of accelerated technological innovation. It relied on factors that have been completely overrun.

As startups such as Uber, Airbnb, Netflix, Tesla, and Amazon—beacons of innovation, public interest, and excitement—began to appear on the scene and eat the s&p 500's lunch, corporate analysts made "innovation" the new mantra. As a result, companies desperately want to accelerate the innovation engine.

While that's fine, I believe there's rarely a lack of good, creative ideas in your company. You should definitely continue to uncover those great ideas, but I don't believe innovation is the problem. In fact, companies treat it just like *Willy Wonka and the Chocolate Factory*. They're opening a million chocolate bars hoping to find the one golden ticket that will send them into the stratosphere.

That approach worked decades ago because everything moved at a slower pace. People were more patient, and the markets could wait while companies tossed out a bunch of ideas and waited for one to click. That approach doesn't work anymore, even though executives still try.

Look at the world of venture capital. The model for getting startup funding has radically changed, and the majority of venture capitalists and firms today won't invest into a business idea until leaders can show that they've prototyped and monetized it. Most people assume if they simply pitch an amazing idea to a group of venture capitalists, they will get the funding they need to start the company, but the vast majority of venture capitalists won't fund an idea, because they know that approach wastes a lot of money. They want to see the prototype up and running, even if it's not yet profitable. They demand evidence that the idea is something people are willing to buy. Only then will they consider funding it.

The majority of venture capital investors have become second-round funders. They no longer want to invest in the initial startup costs, because the risk is too high. The risk-to-reward model doesn't pan out for first-round investors, so investors want to know that the general public is willing to buy your product or service before they will invest.

You can't throw a million ideas out there and cross your fingers, hoping that one of them will take off. That strategy of hope doesn't generate the earnings that people demand. If it's not about innovation, what's it about?

It's about executing those ideas. It's about measuring execution capability at the point of decision so you know you can move a great idea forward and achieve success. Where does this measurement get injected into the decision-making process? Let's take a look.

THE STAGES OF THE DECISION PROCESS

You need to develop pinpoint accuracy in your decision process so that when you settle on an idea, everyone can move forward together, confident that you possess the means to implement it. Everyone should have clarity as to why the decision was made to move forward on this particular initiative in the first place.

You're harvesting data from your own people in order to answer that question, because the answers are there. You've already invested a lot of money in your human capital process: recruiting, onboarding, and retention. Now you are harvesting the fruits of that investment and extracting its value.

Think about it this way. If you have 200,000 people working for you, you have 200,000 people's worth of insight just waiting to be leveraged as a hive mind. In the process, you acquire data about the nimbleness of your organization, your ability to adapt and move forward, and you identify any bottlenecks or roadblocks.

Ultimately, an execution capability score is a data collection system. You are harvesting data about your adaptability out of your own business on a daily basis, like a front-end real-time app. In that way, it's not unlike Facebook or Spotify, both of which also collect data on a continual basis about users.

In a similar way, measuring execution capability actively collects data on your business's ability to adapt to strategy in the next six, nine, twelve, and eighteen months, providing root capability data that you would otherwise have no insight about. No longer do you have to rely on the opinions of executives. Assumption and guesswork are replaced by hard facts and clear data.

When a problem comes out of the woodwork, you're no longer relying on your executive team to assess the threat and find a path to either remove or minimize the impact. When you start collecting data, the patterns will begin to emerge, revealing which functions or units are preventing you from moving forward. You now have something quantifiable to add into your decision-making process.

What does the typical decision process look like?

FIRST STAGE: IDEATION

When you have a market demand, operations begin to kick up ideas to leadership, creating initiative to feed an overall strategy that will meet the demand. Executives gather these ideas, spreading them on the table like cards in a poker game, and wonder which one, which lucky one, will make all the difference.

SECOND STAGE: ANALYSIS

These ideas then go through an executive analysis process. In most companies, the originators of the ideas become annoyed at how long it takes to get through the approval process. It can easily take nine months or more. This frustrates the originators, it frustrates the business units, it frustrates the executives—it frustrates everybody.

Everyone is stuck in lockdown while executives try to figure out which one is a good idea, and if the economics make sense, because they know if it doesn't work, the board will come back and say, "Why are you funding these terrible projects? What was your process for deciding to fund them?"

THIRD STAGE: APPROVAL

Eventually, executives get to the approval process, but it's purely bias-driven. It's Willy Wonka's golden ticket all over again. "Let's go ahead and unwrap this chocolate bar. Maybe it will have a golden ticket." In reality, they're just tossing the dice and saying, "We've got a good feeling about this one."

That's why GE is no longer in the S&P 500. They gambled on uncertain initiatives too many times. They tossed the dice and lost more often than they won. It's the same reason Hewlett Packard sold off its consulting group. Bias-driven decisions have a bad win rate. Very few chocolate bars have golden tickets hiding under the wrapper, but executives keep buying them until it becomes untenable.

There are countless stories in the corporate world of companies driven into the ground because they didn't understand their execution capability. They saw big numbers but didn't understand that the cost would be even bigger. An idea spends nine or more months in the analysis process, and by the time it finally gets approved, executives still have no idea if their teams can successfully implement it.

A BETTER DECISION PROCESS

Rather than going through these stages—ideation, analysis, approval—start looking at execution capability.

Save yourself those nine months of analysis by inject-ing this information early enough in the decision pro-cess that you can recognize an idea that won't work right away. "This is a solid idea, but we won't be able to execute it at this time." If you still believe it's the right idea, then you can say, "In order to get there, we will first have to remove some obstacles in our business. Do we have the money to do that?"

This narrow pool of better initiatives accelerates your strategies because you know you're always fully ready. There are no hidden vulnerabilities that will surprise you, trip you up, or slow you down. It's a streamlined and super-focused decision process that moves for-ward at a high clip.

What if you're forced to move on an initiative because of a change in the market, or you have to get something done within a certain time constraint even though you still have obstacles in the way? If your execution capa-bility measurement reveals that you're in a poor position to move on an obligatory initiative, you at least know enough to delay moving forward on other initiatives. Since you know up front that it's going to consume more time and resources, you can divert the time and resources from other initiatives before it becomes a problem.

In McKinsey's global survey on strategic decision-making, researchers learned that "companies where executives rate their strategic decisions overall as good, they are much likelier than others to say the company's assessment of its own capability to carry out the particular decision was realistic, regardless of whether this decision had a good or bad outcome...Indeed, at companies with good overall processes, realistic assessment of execution capabilities is the third highest-rated activity, regardless of whether the particular decision had a satisfactory outcome."[28]

A LAYER CAKE OF PROCESS

To understand where measuring execution capability fits into your decision process, think of a layer cake. Everyone wants to move from the first layer, which is ideation, directly to the third layer, which is approval. They are missing the middle layer, which is the execution capability measurement.

In the absence of this measurement, they try to analyze an idea using a mishmash of previous projects,

---

28 "Flaws in strategic decision making: McKinsey Global Survey results," *McKinsey & Company, January* 2009, https://www. mckinsey.com/business-functions/strategy-and-corporate-finance/our-insights/flaws-in-strategic-decision-making-mckinsey-global-survey-results.

believing that past success and failure will reveal best practices. That might work to some degree if you were operating in a vacuum, but no company operates in a vacuum. There are too many changing conditions that get continually introduced. No approach is completely static. Even two initiatives that are practically identical will experience different conditions as they are executed.

Maybe you've experienced this. You implemented a product launch and everything went perfectly. Then you implemented a second, very similar product launch, and it flew off the rails. Maybe these two launches occurred at the same time. What do executives do in that case? They often say, "We'd better take some people and resources from the good project and move it over to the failing project. That will fix it." In reality, it only marginally impacts the failing project. Even though these two product launches were almost identical in the beginning, a lot of variation is always in play. You can't assume one will succeed because the other did.

ReM Score™ would have identified the different conditions and context, making it clear that one project would probably fail. You would have known that there was nothing you could do to make it work. Bad meat is bad meat. You can try to cover it up with a bunch of sauce and spices, but it's still bad meat and will probably make you sick. Even a good project under bad conditions shouldn't move forward if you don't have the ability to execute it.

Put the middle layer back into the cake. Introduce execution capability measurement very early into your decision process, so you can pour all of your resources into initiatives that you know will produce good results. It might sound bold, but this measurement works every single time for every single strategic initiative. It's not something you just sprinkle into your process. It should become institutional to your process, so that nothing moves forward without it.

This will align the people generating ideas, the people approving them, and the people executing them. No longer will these three groups feel disconnected, or view one another as a hindrance, danger, or source of frustration. Everyone will know that any idea that is proposed, funded, and put into action has an excellent chance of success. To put it bluntly, nobody is being asked to polish a rock and turn it into gold.

It's like finding the *real* golden ticket without wasting resources purchasing and unwrapping thousands of chocolate bars.

But what exactly is the real golden ticket?

CHAPTER 8

HARVESTING DATA GOLD

When you're an executive, the true golden ticket isn't merely being able to execute on a strategic initiative. It's isn't just about making a winning decision. It's data.

Data is the golden ticket you've been looking for all along, whether you realized it or not. It gives you the ability to execute individual initiatives that support your overall strategy. By measuring each strategic initiative, running ReM Scores™ for each one, you aggregate execution data that helps you fully understand your business. You gain a clear sense of what the vulnerabilities are in each part of your business, which parts are doing well at the moment, and which ones are restricting the fulfillment of your needs.

This overall view enables you to adjust your strategy to shifting market conditions, and empowers C-suite executives to see the tipping point when a particular operating unit within the company needs to change a mission, skillset, or leadership to get ready for the next version of the company.

When you run an execution capability score, you're aggregating data about your business, which allows you to find the proper balance between operational optimization and your ability to adapt to market shift. As Netflix has learned, if you turn the screws too far in one direction, then you won't be able to adapt to market shifts. You will find yourself frozen in your current position by rigid processes.

What Netflix points out in their presentation is that company leaders often feel trapped between chaos and order. They tighten their processes to avoid the chaos, and in so doing, make their companies inflexible and unable to move. Ultimately, Netflix has decided to compensate for this by hiring high-performance people. They lean heavily on their recruiting capacity.[29]

That's the solution they've adopted in response to the data they've collected within their own organization. They've learned an important lesson—you don't have to turn to an outside expert to gain insight about your own company. All of that insight already exists inside the company. You just have to harvest it.

YOUR FUTURE IS IN YOUR DATA

By having the data collected in a structured and deliberate way that's directly correlated to existing initiatives, you gain precision in understanding the specifics of your company. Now you can see exactly what is helping you move forward, initiative by initiative, and what is holding you back.

When you begin gathering this data during the ideation phase, you avoid wasting time and resources. You don't waste time trying to get an initiative approved that is doomed, and you avoid getting somewhere into

---

29 "Netflix Culture: Freedom and Responsibility," *Netflix,* https://
    jobs.netflix.com/culture, accessed February 22, 2019.

your execution phase before realizing you have to cut ties and call it a loss.

You create an active data process that is constantly informing you about your readiness to move to the next level of your strategy. The data also protects you from ideas that sound amazing but can't be realized at the present time. Sometimes, executives get tempted by an amazing idea and, in the absence of data, the temptation proves too much. "This has to work," they say. "It's just so good!" With execution capability data, you will be able to say, "This idea sounds good, but we can't move forward on this, not in our present state. We just don't have the support structure."

When your company comes to a fork in the road, you won't get stuck, unsure which way to go, having no idea which one will lead to success and which to ruin. Instead, the constant data coming from within your organization will provide clear vision and direction when you reach those decision points.

When you have a specific destination in mind, the data will help you understand the timeframe your company needs to get there and the cost structure that will be necessary in order to benefit earnings per share. In the absence of guesswork, your strategy will begin to build steam and accelerate.

HARVESTING AND USING DATA

Let's look at the actual step-by-step process for harvesting and using the data from within your organization.

ELIMINATE DATA BIAS

First, eliminate the bias that says either the data doesn't exist or the data resides purely in past performance. Reject the notion that data is only relevant within the primary unit that it comes from. For example, just because you are implementing a technology project doesn't mean relevant data only comes from IT. Just because you're doing an acquisition doesn't mean relevant data only comes from finance or HR. Just because you're launching a new product doesn't mean relevant data only comes from focus groups.

COLLECT DATA FROM THE FOURTEEN DOMAINS

You have to begin embracing a wider and deeper understanding of where relevant data comes from, because resources are rarely siloed. People working in a specific part of the business will usually touch on other parts of the business from time to time. With any initiative, some degree of overlap always takes place.

This is the reason for the fourteen domains. Now that you've embraced that broader view, it's time to collect data across all of them. Companies mistakenly believe they can't find the data they need to measure what matters internally, so they turn to external sources. Resist the temptation to do this. All of the information you need to measure the fourteen domains will come from within your organization. You have untapped resources for harvesting that data in your teams.

RESIST RELYING ON HISTORICAL PERFORMANCE DATA

You also have to resist the urge to turn to historical performance data to guide your decision. Stick to the domains and fight the temptation to look to the past to inform the future. It's a common bias among executives to assume that historical data is the only concrete data. This is completely wrong. The *only* time that historical performance data *might* be relevant is when you're running an initiative that is *exactly* the same as one you've done in the past.

This rarely happens, which is why companies wind up with Frankenstein models comprised of bits of pieces from past projects. Leaders are trying to mitigate unknown risks, but a Frankenstein project should never move forward. If the project is absolutely essential, then everyone should at least be clear up front that it's going to be a nightmare effort. Other initiatives will have to be set aside, so extra resources can be committed to this nightmare initiative. It won't be fun, but it's better if everyone goes into it with eyes wide open. Your company is more likely to get through it if you know it's going to be a rough ride.

AGGREGATE THE DATA

You are collecting the data for one specific initiative at a time, but it's important to aggregate this data. As you gather all this data from various initiatives on an ongoing basis, you will gain insight on the ability of your business to quickly adapt to the next iteration of strategy. This aggregation of data also gives you a clear sense of every operation and division within your company, so you know exactly where each bottleneck, weakness, and vulnerability are located. This knowledge, in turn, enables you to make more strategic and tactical decisions.

In the end, you no longer have to play the guessing game or tolerate failure. That tolerance won't exist anymore, because you will have a clear picture of your company's ability to execute initiatives. With execution capability measurement data, you know your weaknesses, you know where you excel, and you know when you need to adapt and transform for the future.

It's the aggregation of data that gives you this broader insight into your company, and it's insight that most executives, even in the largest corporations, have never had. Even today, with all of our tools for creating metrics, most corporate executives still don't have this insight. They are still taking significant leaps of faith or making major assumptions when trying to get a broad picture of the company, using their own experience and knowledge to fill in the gaps.

With this aggregation of data, which you continue to collect with every initiative, you are always in a position to adapt your business to changing needs. You are never caught off guard by a shifting market, unsure of how to respond, because you maintain that deep understanding of your execution capability at all times.

DISCOVERING UNTAPPED INSIGHTS

ReM Score™ works. It shows you the bottlenecks and vulnerabilities. It enables you to make better strategic and tactical decisions, so you never find yourself half-way through a project and realize you've veered way off course. No longer will you find yourself in a situation where you have to spend a ton of extra time and money to restructure an entire operating unit to keep an initiative in process from failing.

As we've said, you already have all the data you need inside your company, because you've already done a great job of building recruiting, training, and retention programs. You probably already hire and retain the best people in the market. It might even be part of your values and mission statement.

There is a lot of untapped insight in your people, and a lot of capability is being underutilized. If you can just clear the vulnerabilities out of the way, you will discover that your people have a much greater capability to help your business grow than you ever imagined.

You've been looking for that golden ticket for years. You've purchased and unwrapped an uncountable number of chocolate bars hoping to find it, and all along, the golden ticket was *already* in your possession. You simply lacked a mechanism to see it.

This metric works because it has been developed from a thousand points of information gleaned from numerous studies, some of which have lasted for two decades and come from multiple originators and many different groups that have studied this issue both academically and as a business model. What this compilation of research has given us is the ability to step back and measure the whole picture of our businesses.

The fourteen domains of measurement are a distillation of the research combined with our own experience. It's the golden ticket you've been looking for. It turns you into a continual data-collection engine, eliminating the obstacles that keep getting in the way and accelerating your strategies, helping you keep pace with the super-pace of today's market. When the next nimble startup appears suddenly on the scene, you will be ready to adapt and meet the challenge.

CONCLUSION

The decision process today is failing executives, but they continue to rely on it because it's all they've known. Though the process has been leveraged for decades in positive ways, the super-pace of the market today, and the unrelenting emergence of startups that erode established companies, are changing that. The current strategic decision-making process has never had to deal with so much change.

The process itself isn't flawed. At one time, it worked well, but it is simply not designed to deal with today's reality. The old executive decision process is coming to the end of its useful life, so leaders in every company need to transition to a model that adds more insight, measuring each individual initiative for execution capability prior to adoption and implementation. This saves companies time and money, but it also provides compounding insight into the company's overall health.

It's a smart idea to cultivate innovation in your company, but when people come to you with innovative ideas, the value of the idea alone isn't enough to move forward with it. You have to offset that decision by measuring execution capability. After all, the best idea in the world is useless if you can't act on it, and even an amazing idea can turn into a nightmare if your team encounters unexpected obstacles.

When it comes to execution capability, your best guess is never enough. Too many leaders make decisions based on assumption. That's like a bank deciding to make a loan based on mere opinion rather than a credit score, or a university admitting a student based on a hunch rather than including their SAT score. Scores such as these exist because people need data to make better decisions.

FUELING YOUR DECISION ENGINE

When you start measuring execution capability on an ongoing business, you begin gathering data to fuel your decision-making engine for the future. You gain the ability to make adjustments internally when swift or unexpected changes hit the market, because you're filtering out the biases that steer you into cash-consuming and time-consuming positions. Without this vital information, all of the programs you've rolled out to increase productivity and employee participation get eroded by an undercurrent of poor execution capability and constant frustration.

Imagine a decision-making process in which you know for a fact whether or not an acquisition is going to work, whether or not a product launch is going to work, or whether or not your back-office modernization is going to work. Imagine a process in which you know your promotion of programs won't be diminished during implementation, because the data has already confirmed that your company can make it happen.

What would it do for the morale of your people if 50 percent of your strategic initiatives were no longer failing? How would it affect the market's perception of your business and leadership if your success rate drifted closer and closer to 100 percent?

You probably already know how frustrating it can be for executives when they're under constant pressure from analysts and investor expectations, as well as the constant appearance of new competitors. As a leader, you've probably dealt with the frustration of handing a great idea to your team only to see them struggle to make it work. You've probably had those difficult conversations where you say, "Why can't you people move this thing further along? Why has this become such a boondoggle?"

When fatigue and discouragement set in, productivity only declines further. People try to halfheartedly manipulate the outcome as best they can to realize better earnings per share, but in the end, the initiative doesn't benefit the business.

The good news is that execution capability can be measured. It's not some elusive butterfly that you have little chance of finding, nor is it merely an opinion. It's a real, accessible database that incorporates all of the relevant factors associated with every type of strategic initiative. It also helps you see the broader perspective on what will impact the outcome of those initiatives.

THE POWER OF ReM SCORE™

ReM Score™ provides a holistic execution capability score that reveals all the factors impacting your company's ability to realize strategic initiatives. Use it right after the ideation process in your decision-making for best results. As soon as someone comes up with a great idea in your company, immediately run a ReM Score™ to see if you can actually execute it.

Even if the idea is only in its conceptual infancy, ReM allows you to accelerate the approval process by giving you the numbers you need to prove you can make it work. You can approve it with confidence and get it to market with speed, increasing your overall market position, because the data tells you so.

If the data reveals otherwise, then you can kill the idea or put it on hold, knowing that you won't waste a lot of time and money on something that won't work. More importantly, you identified the vulnerabilities in your company that are preventing the implementation of great ideas, so you can begin to address and remove them.

This clears the way for future innovation, making an execution capability score a decision accelerator that picks up speed as the data aggregates. In that way, it's about more than the individual initiatives, it's also about tuning your business along the way thanks to your continuous data harvesting.

THE TIPPING POINT

Let me encourage you to try a different approach this time. During the next round of ideation, put on the brakes and inject execution capability into the process right then. Measure your execution capability using the fourteen domains listed in this book. Do this for at least the top five, possibly the top ten, initiatives on the table.

Once you have measured them, use that information to guide your decision-making, narrowing your focus to those initiatives that have the greatest chance of success based on the data. Begin to operationalize this measurement into your approval process, and you will begin to see a much greater success rate.

Then take a step back and aggregate the data. What has the data revealed about your organization? Where are the vulnerabilities that need to be corrected? The hardest part of this will be trusting the scores that come back, but it's important to remember that ReM is based on research and analysis. It's not an opinion.

As you begin using the data to identify and correct vulnerabilities, your company's ability to successfully implement great ideas will improve. Your process will become more streamlined, and you will learn to trust what the data tells you. At that point, you can begin allowing your people to rely on it more comfortably as you introduce more initiatives. You can even begin to dream bigger, because you have accelerated your execution.

ReM contributes to a scaling up process, as the data creates a feedback loop that produces constant refinement. After several months or quarters of data collection, your business will become a self-correcting machine, capable of greater, faster, and more effective idea implementation than you ever thought possible.

APPENDIX

GO WITH CONFIDENCE

The topic of this book isn't entirely new. However, the existing research has never been synthesized into a single easy-to-operationalize model that removes personal biases and delivers the data as a single metric to help you in your decision process for each individual initiative you are considering.

For nearly sixty years, economists and psychologists have been working to understand why we make the decisions we do, especially the decisions that are made by those who run companies. Behavioral economics, as it is known, combines the cognitive models of decision-making with the economic models of rational behavior. The research is extensive, deep, and varied. Consequently, so are the results and explanations.

In the past twenty years, the focus of this research has shifted and narrowed, seeking to understand more about the impact that decisions (both good and bad) have on a business's ability to grow and sustain its growth across varying economic conditions. With this shifting focus, even more studies have gained insights about how behavior affects decision making.

This research inspired me to find the root cause of why an initiative goes well or poorly. The bottom line, I found, is that it all starts at the decision point of whether or not to move forward. The largest gap in that process is in understanding your own abilities as a company to do the thing you want to do.

What became most clear is that executives largely overestimate the capabilities of their own companies to deliver a strategy, and they tend to use biases rather than data to make the final decision to move forward. When I studied this closely, I found that no one was measuring that specific factor in the equation.

Understanding how to measure execution capability came from a lot of research and a variety of sources, some from my own global consulting work and others from published volumes of research on this topic. Below, I have provided some of the key reference materials that hit high points of insight. Although there is quite a bit more—most of which is easy to find and access through simple online searches—these will provide a reading list for those interested in a deeper dive.

Why Decisions Fail: Avoiding the Blunders and Traps That Lead to Debacles by Paul C. Nutt (Berrett-Koehler Publishers, 2002).

"Closing the Gap Between Strategy and Execution" by Donald Sull, MIT *Sloan Management Review*, July 1, 2007.

Thinking, Fast and Slow by Daniel Kahneman (Farrar, Straus and Giroux, 2001).

"Root Out Bias from Your Decision-Making Process," Thomas C. Redman, *Harvard Business Review*, March 10, 2017.

"Noise: How to Overcome the High, Hidden Cost
of Inconsistent Decision Making," by Daniel
Kahneman, Andrew M. Rosenfield, Linnea Gandhi,
and Tom Blaser, *Harvard Business Review*, October
2016.

"Outsmart Your Own Biases," by Jack B. Soll,
Katherine L. Milkman, and John W. Payne, *Harvard
Business Review*, May 2015.

"Identifying the Biases Behind Your Bad Decisions,"
by John Beshears and Francesca Gino, *Harvard
Business Review*, October 31, 2014.

"To Avoid Confirmation Bias in your Decisions,
Consider the Alternatives," by JM Olejarz, *Harvard
Business Review*, July 5, 2017.

"Flaws in Strategic Decision Making: McKinsey Global
Survey," by Renee Dye, Olivier Sibony, and Vincent
Truong, *McKinsey & Company*, January 2009.

"The Secrets to Successful Strategy Execution," by
Gary L. Neilson, Karla L. Martin, and Elizabeth
Powers, *Harvard Business Review*, June 2008.

Louis Rosenberg, David Baltaxe, Niccolo Pescetelli, "Crowds vs swarms, a comparison of intelligence," *2016 Swarm/Human Blended Intelligence Workshop (SHBI)*, pp. 1-4, 2016.

Louis Rosenberg, "Human swarming, a real-time method for parallel distributed intelligence," *2015 Swarm/Human Blended Intelligence Workshop (SHBI)*, pp. 1–7, 2015.

Louis Rosenberg, Niccolo Pescetelli, "Amplifying prediction accuracy using Swarm A.I." *2017 Intelligent Systems Conference (IntelliSys)*, pp. 61–65, 2017.

Mohammad Majid al-Rifaie, John Mark Bishop, "Swarm intelligence and weak artificial creativity," *The Association for the Advancement of Artificial Intelligence (AAAI)*, 2013.

ACKNOWLEDGMENTS

I tend to think out loud. More specifically, I process out loud, which means people who spend any significant amount of time with me have to hear me talk about the topic of this book incessantly—a problem that has occasionally fallen into the category of "Alexsplaining" when I'm at my worst.

It took seven—yes, *seven*—years for me to finally write this book, so I would first like to recognize all the poor bastards I have drug through the process and who, thankfully and very graciously, have been patient with me and lent their contributions, so I could do this.

Thank you.

(By the way, now you get to hear me talk about the book, so congratulations—no good deed goes unpunished.)

THE LIST

For the person out there who once told me, "If it isn't written down, it doesn't exist."

To I.C. and R.C., two people who embody the best this world can be. Thank you for your unwavering support and belief in me.

To M.M., thank you for listening and pushing me past the tipping point of getting this book done. Your support and enthusiasm gave me what I needed when I needed it.

To Lonnie Martin, my mentor and friend, for your bull-shit meter and calling me "captain" when you could have easily used many other "titles." Thank you for helping me find the path to get this done, for your constant clear and precise feedback, and the patience to stick with and guide me to this point. Your insights have been relevant, grounding, and powerful.

To my friend and business partner, C.C., for pointing at me and laughing every time I would talk about this model for the first five years. You played me like a fiddle, it worked, and now here it is.

To the clients who have shared their stories, frustrations, and enthusiasm for finding a better way. I am grateful to you all for your generosity.

To the leadership of TaxAudit.com and CalPERS who, as early adopters, embraced what this model can do and provided the generous and vital feedback toward improving the process and platform.

To EMRL, especially Floyd and Stephen, for your continued support and excitement in developing and marketing this model and platform.

To James, Jeff, Karla and the rest of the team at Scribe. I could not have asked for a better team of people to help in writing this book. Its success comes from how well you captured and structured my thoughts. Its failure is all your fault.

ABOUT THE AUTHOR

Alex Castro is the CEO of M Corp and has helped clients deliver complex corporate strategies for the last twenty years. He finds new approaches to serving and building companies by identifying their operational vulnerabilities and correcting them, and the ReM Score™ has evolved from hundreds of engagements into a digital platform tool. Alex is a graduate of Northeastern University, where he was a collegiate rower, and he later went on to coach the University of California-Davis rowing team. He is also an avid mountain biker and has two wonderful daughters who are a constant source of inspiration and joy.

Made in the USA
Monee, IL
14 September 2021